SOCIOLOGICAL CONCEPTS

AND RESEARCH

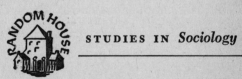

STUDIES IN *Sociology*

SOCIOLOGICAL CONCEPTS AND RESEARCH

*Acquisition, Analysis, and Interpretation
of Social Information*

Ralph Thomlinson
California State College at Los Angeles

RANDOM HOUSE
New York

Third Printing, November 1966

Library of Congress Catalog Card Number: 65-13763

MANUFACTURED IN THE UNITED STATES OF AMERICA

Preface

*

Being the last part of a book to be written, the preface has the curious property of offering the author an opportunity to state intentions after his work has been completed. This short volume is intended as a quick survey of how modern sociologists go about their daily chores. Anticipated uses include: supplement to an introductory text for instructors wanting to stress empiricism, introduction to advanced courses in methodology and statistics, review-refresher for students studying for comprehensive examinations, and something to recommend to general readers to indicate what contemporary sociology is all about. Profundity, originality, and thoroughness are sacrificed to serve these purposes, though some intellectual maturity is assumed. No topic is covered completely; for further reading, see the appended bibliography and especially the footnoted citations, most of which are included primarily to direct interested readers to relevant writings rather than merely to serve as academic documentation.

Preparation of this book has benefited from my teachers, especially those in departments in which I majored (philosophy, city planning, and sociology) or minored (mathematics, physics, psychology, geography, and anthropology) at Oberlin College, Yale University, University of Pittsburgh, Harvard University, Montclair State College, New School for Social Research, and Columbia University. I also owe thanks to my colleagues and students in sociology and other departments at the University of Wisconsin at Madison, Denison University, California State College at Los Angeles, the Bureau of Applied Social Research at Columbia University, and the Actuarial Department of Metropolitan Life Insurance Company.

The actual writing also owes much of its quality (and none of its defects) to others. Herman J. Loether and Charles H. Page read drafts of the manuscript and suggested improvements, Margaret W. Thomlinson supplied clerical aid, and the Random House staff added useful recommendations.

R. T.

Contents

SOCIOLOGICAL CONCEPTS
AND RESEARCH

⌣

Basic Sociological Concepts

✳

What is this thing called sociology? Devotees of Cole Porter and Mozart may resent the impertinent paraphrase,[1] but the question has been made intellectually pertinent by the growing interest in the social sciences. Since World War II, the young discipline named sociology has been gaining a stronger and stronger niche in the halls of academe. Yet many people still do not know just what this young subject is.

Sociology is popularly stereotyped as an attempt to alleviate problems associated with the four D's: drink, drugs, drainage, and divorce. This gutter-ameliorative attitude is frequently a motive for taking a course in sociology, but it rarely suffices to maintain an abiding interest in the subject—for two reasons.

First, professional sociologists are more interested in normal than in abnormal behavior—although the latter gets more publicity. In our efforts to understand human thoughts and actions, we study marriage more extensively than divorce, law-abiders before criminals, trust rather than hostility, sobriety in preference to alcoholism, well-adjusted persons instead of psychoneurotic patients, and peace sooner than war.

Second, professional sociologists devote more time and energy to ascertaining the facts concerning human behavior than to trying to alter these facts. True, many sociologists share with other people the desire to direct mankind toward some intellectual or emotional ideal, but the discipline of sociology discourages such efforts in favor of learning what are the present ideals and observing the extent to which overt behavior approaches these standards. One objective of graduate work in sociology is to channel the passion of the do-gooder into a competence in fact-finding research.

People in Groups

The purpose of sociology is to understand people's (and one's own) thoughts and actions by putting them into the perspective gained by knowledge of other people in other groups (non-Western societies, different social classes, contrasting families, and so forth), and by recognizing the groups of which one is a member and tracing their impact on oneself (societies, classes, families, and other groups). Thus sociology is the study of people in groups—a delineation of the influence of groups on individual behavior, personality, and thinking, as well as, in turn, the influence of individuals on groups.

An historically important instance of the contribution to be made by sociological analysis was supplied by Émile Durkheim's 1897 book on suicide.[2] Before publication of this early sociological classic, most people assumed that the occurrence of suicide was best explained by examining the temperament of the individual, looking for evidence of neurasthenia, insanity, alcoholism, hereditary defect, and the like. Some preferred to explain suicide on the basis of such social factors as financial insolvency or political insecurity, or as the result of such physical phenomena as temperature, moon phases, and sun spots. Durkheim's contribution was to introduce sociological factors: marital

status, education, degree of individuation, religion, social cohesion, and the like. His statistical techniques
were crude by modern standards, yet this pioneer
sociologist was able to show the significance of the
types and strengths of the relations individuals have
with groups and group-endorsed values and attitudes.

Sociology, in short, is a complement of psychology.
Psychology begins with the individual and then segments him into components; sociology relates the individual to groups. Psychologists analyze the single
human being, whereas sociologists analyze the group.
Psychology is the study of the constituent make-up of
the person; sociology is the study of the person within
organizations. These organizations vary in size, character, and degree of influence—from the intimate clique
or close-knit family to the nation or society.

Society and Culture

A society is a large, continuing, organized group of
people; it is the fundamental large-scale human group.
A culture is the total way of life of the people—the
way they behave and think. Culture is that part of our
environment that is man-made, as opposed to the natural environment. It is impossible to gain a thorough
comprehension of the behavior of any person or animal unless we know what his social life is like. In sum,
to understand an action requires knowledge of its context.

Culture has three aspects: technological, sociological, and ideological. 1) In man's struggle to wrest from
his habitat the various necessary means of subsistence,
he makes artifacts or physical objects. The material
side of culture includes his tools, clothing, shelter,
weapons, and so on. It also includes the techniques
for the use of these artifacts. 2) The category of socio-
facts or social organization includes the various group-
ings into families, clubs, religious sects, fraternities,
and many others. This aspect also covers the economic

and political structure. Culture is manifested through the social organization and the people in it. 3) The value system refers to the way of looking at life— philosophical tenets, religious beliefs, and rules of behavior. Values are beliefs upon which people build their lives. Major American values are success, efficiency, progress, material comfort, equality, freedom, nationalism, conformity, and democracy.[3]

Within a culture, there may be subcultures. A subculture is a variant of the larger culture of which it forms a part. Members of groups that have subcultures share their own characteristic ways of acting and thinking. As in linguistics, just as dialects are mutually comprehensible variants of a language, so subcultures are sufficiently closely related to the dominant culture to permit social interaction, but yet different enough to require special effort to achieve mutual comprehension. Examples of subcultures are the French Canadians in Quebec and the plantation South of the United States. In some cases, the subculture is distinguished by elements of conflict or criminal deviation, as for example the adolescent peer subculture[4] and the boy's gang.[5] Subcultures, like cultures, have normative behavioral standards to which members are expected to conform.

Social Norms

Norms are rules in the game of life. It is through social norms and values that the interpersonal relations of members of a society are controlled and directed, usually without the awareness of the persons who are conforming. One intent of sociology is to make us aware of these and other forces that motivate us and our associates.

These "rules" are of four types: techniques, folkways, mores, and laws. Techniques are ways of doing things where the criterion is technical efficiency. Folkways are "correct" ways of doing things; the keynote is etiquette. Mores (singular: mos) are like folkways except that a stronger moral value is involved. Laws are formal means to social control, made explicit through codification.

We may contrast these four types of norms by considering what happens when a person violates each one. If one does not follow a technique, he is simply considered inefficient or wasteful; aside from his boss or wife, no one is offended. A person who violates a folkway is socially disapproved through the imposition of some mild sanction such as a dirty look or temporary severance of informal neighborhood social relations. Violation of a mos brings down a severe informal penalty, such as complete social ostracism. Breaking a law calls forth punishment by formal authorities, but the punishment need not be necessarily severe.

To illustrate these differences, consider care of the lawn by suburbanites. The technique aspect involves questions of whether a power mower is better than a hand mower, or what is the best pattern of cutting: circular, rectangular, in strips, or otherwise. A common suburban folkway is that lawns must be cut once a week; another, that the husband should cut the lawn (especially when a power mower is used). In some communities, wives and children may mow, or lawns may not be cut on Sunday. A mowing mos is violated when the weeds get to be taller than the iris, or when the man forces his wife to cut the lawn the day after she returns from the hospital with the new baby. Local laws may prohibit sprinkling on Monday, Wednesday, or Friday during a water shortage. But whereas failure to obey the law may be condoned or even encouraged by neighbors as long as no folkway or mos is violated, deviating from the mores may cause a neighbor to telephone the police even if no law is broken. Sometimes people are put in the position of being forced to violate either the law or the mores (group-induced "I dare you" pranks, for example).

Of these four kinds of customs in the sociological analysis of human behavior, folkways and mores are the most important. It was the primacy of mores over laws that caused Sumner to entitle one of his chapters "The Mores Can Make Anything Right and Prevent Condemnation of Anything."[6] To quote a modern essayist, "The vanity of lawyers in assuming that the law has a significant effect on sexual habits is matched by the vanity of writers in assuming that literature has a comparable effect."[7]

A fashion (and its *a fortiori* companion, fad) is a folkway of temporary duration, widely adopted in the society or community, not supported by formal social control, and sometimes recurring periodically. To cite one of many available examples, two anthropologists measured six dimensions of European women's clothing over three centuries (length of skirt, length of waist, depth of decolletage, width of skirt, thickness of waist, and width of decolletage), concluding that such stylistic features alternate between maximum and minimum measurements on an average of every 50 years, for an over-all periodicity or total wave length of around a century.[8] Fashion also appears to play a role in reproductive behavior: at some times and in certain groups, it is fashionable to have no children; at other times, the small family is popular; at still other times, the more the merrier.

Understanding social norms helps to avoid the semantic fallacy of confusing the label with its referent. Labels are apt to be legally defined; folkways and mores reflect actual usage. For instance, residents of a community may delude themselves into believing that their town is not racially segregated because there are no formal laws requiring separation of races, whereas the community may have a rigid *de facto* system of segregation which everyone follows, no one dares subvert, and no one proclaims publicly.

Status and Role

Associated with these social norms are sets of ranked and unranked statuses and their roles or expected behavior. A person's status is his position in a group, often defined in terms of how others treat him. Every person has many statuses, one for each group in which he participates. And for each status, there is a corresponding role. A person's role is what he is expected to do; it is the dynamic or functional aspect of status.

Status and role are useful and convenient, for they make social life easy. By providing recognizable niches and correlative sets of rights, duties, and mutual expectations, they smooth social relations. And since nearly everyone acts to a large extent in accord with his designated role, reinforcement is frequent. Those who deviate from their appointed roles may be called Bohemians or beatniks, according to the year.

Two kinds of statuses may be distinguished. Ascribed statuses are assigned to individuals without allowance for their innate differences or abilities; achieved statuses are filled through competition and individual effort.[9] Ascribed statuses are based ordinarily on age, sex, family, or caste; achieved statuses may be founded on talent, education, or publicity. Many achievable statuses are in fact severely limited by unacknowledged ascribed prerequisites; for example, the United States presidency is achievable, but not at present by people whose ascribed status is Oriental, Negro, Jew, or female. Young and changing societies have the most achieved statuses. However, even in a relatively open society, ascribed statuses generally outnumber achieved positions.

One reason why these statuses, roles, and norms are so well accepted and why their behavioral dictates are so well conformed to is that most people are trained by parents and peers to accept the existing local situation as normal, natural, and inevitable.

Socialization

Socialization is the process whereby the individual is molded into a social being through learning to think and behave according to the values and norms prevalent in his society. It is how a person becomes a part of a society. Without socialization, the individual has extremely limited capabilities, as is attested by studies of isolated children. "Most of the human behavior we regard as somehow given in the species does not occur apart from training and example by others. Most of the mental traits we think of as constituting the human mind are not present unless put there by communicative contact with others."[10] This dependency on the group is not peculiar to human beings. "It is hardly an exaggeration to say that a chimpanzee kept in solitude is not a real chimpanzee at all."[11]

The complex set of attitudes, habits, and other traits comprising personality owes a great deal to socialization. G. H. Mead insisted that human beings are endowed with personalities by their society and that we are the products rather than the creators of that society. "The organized community or social group . . . gives to the individual his unity of self."[12]

This learning of the standards of expected behavior is akin to psychological conditioning. Children learn through an informal and largely unconscious system of reinforcement and punishment. The primary agent of socialization is the family, although peer groups, the school, and other agencies are often important. Charles A. Beard appropriately called mothers the "constant carriers of common culture."

A well-socialized person internalizes the norms of his society. The result is a powerful instrument of social control operating through conscience, guilt, and other subjective reactions that arise when the socialized person engages in nonconformist actions or is tempted to do so. "Our strongest sentiments of approval or abhorrence are given to us by the age and group in which we live."[13]

Types of Groups

If groups play such an indispensable part in the social maturation of the individual, then it is important to consider what kinds of groups there are. Sociologists distinguish primary from secondary groups. Primary groups are characterized by intimate face-to-face association. They are fundamental in forming the behavior and ideas of the individual. Intimate association creates a fusion of individualities in a common whole, so that, in the words of Charles H. Cooley, the founder of the concept of primary groups, "one's very self, for many purposes at least, is the common life and purpose of the group. Perhaps the simplest way of describing this wholeness is by saying that it is a 'we'; it involves the sort of sympathy and mutual identification for which 'we' is the natural expression."[14] Secondary groups and secondary relationships are simply those that are not primary.

Groups or associations may be vocational (American Medical Association), political (Young Republicans), religious (missionary societies), educational (The Reading Club), recreational (bowling club), ameliorative (Helping Hand Society), or fraternal (Masons). Although some are formal and others informal, all groups have leaders and most impute official or unofficial recognition of status differentials and role expectations of members.

Contrasting to the membership group is the reference group.[15] Instead of the formal physical joining that is the criterion of membership groups, reference groups are based on the internalization of values. A reference group is one to which a person relates himself or to which he aspires to relate himself. It is highly influential in forming a person's values and orienting his behavior. The individual adopts in substantial degree the norms and perspectives of the group. These groups are potent forces for socialization. When a person refers himself to a group to which he aspires, he indulges in *anticipatory socialization.* Take, for example, the medical student prominently displaying his first stethoscope; anticipating the status of "doctor," he is playing the role, albeit prematurely. This concept was used to explain a curious paradox discovered during World War II: "The *less* the promotion opportunity afforded by a branch or a combination of branches, the *more favorable* the opinion tends to be toward promotion opportunity."[16] Here sociologists use the idea of *relative deprivation.* If nearly everyone is promoted, soldiers expect promotion and are likely to complain that their own progress is too slow; where promotions are rare, the soldier is pleased when promoted and relatively uncomplaining when not promoted (we are all doomed together).

The most important primary group, both membership and reference, is the family, by virtue of its universal prevalence, the closeness of its internal relationships, and its preeminence during the formative years of the individual. "The one fact stands out beyond all others that everywhere the husband, wife, and immature children constitute a unit apart from the remainder of the community."[17] Historically, probably the most important secondary group has been the social class or caste.

Social Stratification

Social stratification refers to a broad grouping of the members of a society into levels or ranks. W. Lloyd Warner defines a social class as the largest group of people whose members have intimate social access to one another, thus forming a small social world or subculture.[18] Warner's criteria of class are family membership, size of income, prestige of occupation, church membership, educational level, location of residence, club membership, type of house, nationality of antecedents, manners and deportment, and dress and speech.

Sociologists have identified the ideological configurations of the three major classes in the United States. Upper class people tend to think in terms of time, idealizing the past and placing great stress on primacy of lineage. In the middle class, moral behavior and money are paramount. The economic insecurity of lower class people makes them conceive of class distinctions in terms of wealth.[19]

"Middle class morality" has become a well-used phrase. It refers to intensive preoccupation with self-improvement and conformity. More than the other classes, middle class people are likely to have their status dependent upon the evaluations of their peers. Hence they are motivated to adopt the clothing styles, moral attitudes, child rearing practices, and other behavior patterns of their judges—the rest of the middle class. An extreme form of this ritualistic conformism can be seen in almost any college sorority house.

When mobility of persons between classes is highly restricted, sociologists apply the term *caste*. Customarily caste augments class; the United States' prevailing open (or semi-open) class system is supplemented by a Negro caste (or semi-caste) containing upper, middle, and lower classes. This basing of caste distinctions upon race is commonplace. A thoroughgoing caste system would contain only ascribed statuses and inherited inequality. In actuality, however, no caste system is completely rigid; even in the classic case of India there has always been some movement up and down the social ladder. Without this and other changes in the social system, disruption may result, affecting the ability of the family, the class, and other social groups to fulfill their customary functions.

Functionalism

The structural-functional approach to the analysis of social behavior was first explicitly developed by anthropologists A. R. Radcliffe-Brown and Bronislaw Malinowski, philologist-Semitist William Robertson Smith, and sociologists Émile Durkheim, Talcott Parsons, and Robert K. Merton. Indeed, functionalist principles have been so thoroughly accepted by American sociologists that it now appears proper to say that structural-functional analysis, at least in the United States, is synonymous with sociological analysis.[20]

Functionalists seek to explain social facts by the ways in which they are related to each other within the social system and by the manner in which they relate to the physical surroundings.[21] Parts of a culture should be understood with reference to the whole. This emphasis on the social matrix evokes Aristotle's idea that one cannot understand the function of the human hand without reference to the whole organism; if one were to discover a hand, not knowing its connection with the human body, he would be unable to comprehend the hand's function (although its structure or morphology might be clear).

Functionalists want to know what needs are fulfilled by each trait in the culture. As the term implies, they are interested in what function or service each element of the culture performs for the survival of the society and its culture. The function of a social element is the contribution it makes to the total social life and the adjustment of members of the group.[22] Society is perceived as a complex system of interrelated components, each fulfilling one or more social needs. The antonyms eufunction and dysfunction refer respectively to those observed consequences which promote the adaptation or adjustment of a given system, and those which lessen the adaptation or adjustment of the system.[23]

Functional analysis helps us to understand the presence and persistence of many social problems. Kingsley Davis began an article on prostitution with the question: "Why does an institution so thoroughly disapproved, so widely outlawed in Western civilization, flourish so universally?" and concluded with the reply that it "performs a function which no other institution fully performs."[24]

Manifest and Latent Functions

Merton distinguishes between manifest and latent functions. Manifest functions are those consequences which are "intended and recognized by participants in the system"; latent functions are "those which are neither intended nor recognized."[25] A manifest function of Swarthmore College is to educate its students; a latent function is to act as a marriage broker. The latent functions of Veblen's "conspicuous consumption" form another case in point.[26]

Distinguishing between manifest and latent functions precludes substitution of naïve moral judgments for sociological analysis. "Moral judgments based entirely on an appraisal of manifest functions of a social structure are 'unrealistic' in the strict sense, i.e., they do not take into account other actual consequences of that structure, consequences which may provide basic social support for the structure"; social reforms which ignore latent functions "invariably do so on pain of suffering acute disappointments and 'boomerang' effects."[27] A Chicago precinct captain explained the latent social welfare functions of political machines:

> When anyone gets into trouble with the law—petty thieving, trouble with a relief investigator—or when he loses his job or is about to be evicted, or when a kid gets in with a bad gang and starts staying out all night, in cases like this it is not the relief agency or social welfare agency that the harassed voter first goes to, but rather to the precinct captain who stands in with the law, who will not talk down to him but will treat him as a friend in need, and who is waiting for him in the local tavern or in the ward Hq, where there is a full-time secretary who knows just who can handle the situation.[28]

A Boston ward leader concurred: "I think that there's got to be in every ward somebody that any bloke can come to—no matter what he's done—and get help. Help, you understand; none of your law and justice, but help."[29] Merton explains the ineffectual character of attempts to "turn the rascals out" by a theorem: "Any attempt to eliminate an existing social structure without providing adequate alternative structures for fulfilling the functions previously fulfilled by the abolished organizations is doomed to failure."[30]

Social Theory

Through years of accumulating such theorems there has evolved a facet of sociology known as social theory —a much abused label signifying a body of principles setting forth the interrelations among various sociological factors. In any field, a theory is an attempt to explain observed phenomena through a set of verified generalizations or hypotheses (or a single hypothesis) stating causes and consequences of given events or conditions; in sociology, the phenomena and explanatory factors are of kinds described throughout this chapter. Since sociological theories explain human behavior by tracing causal sequences, they lend themselves to prediction of behavior.

As the next chapter indicates, theorizing is not inherently verbal. The naïve convention that anything not quantified is *ipso facto* theoretical is dangerously misleading. Theories must be couched in clearly defined terms, rigorously ordered; and there is no medium of expression better equipped for precise definitions and exacting instructions than mathematics. Hence social theory may be stated in mathematical terms. In fact, it cannot be overemphasized that a theory is not just a loose accumulation of verbal speculations; theories frequently are quantitative and always must be stringently reasoned and empirically confirmed. Maturation of a discipline into a science demands convergence of empirical and theoretical interests to the point of fusion.

Many theoretical propositions are expressed statistically, in terms of probabilities rather than absolutes —as tendencies instead of certainties. To be sure, sociologists sometimes are able to say: if A, then B, without fail; but more often they must say: if A, then B, 84

per cent of the time. It is on such slipping sands of uncertainty—but definable, measurable, and in a probabilistic sense, predictable uncertainty—that all scientific
edifices are constructed, including physics and sociology.

Mystery and Understanding

Turning toward the other end of the academic spec-
trum, sociology shares with music and poetry the lia-
bility inspired by the layman's belief that thorough,
detailed analysis is antithetical to true appreciation.
This false assumption frequently obscures the fundamental fact that far from interfering with appreciation
of poetic beauty and human idiosyncracies, analysis
(whether scientific or not) is essential to real understanding. Knowing specifically why a poem is emo-
tionally effective is requisite to attainment of a high
order of reading skill. Similarly, comprehension of the
mechanics—both crude and convoluted—of social interaction adds substantially to one's ability to communi-
cate and to participate in the social activities of other
human beings.

The phraseology is a give-away: analyzing poetry
or lovely women or interpersonal relations is said to
"take all the mystery out of it." But that is precisely
what any scholarly subject is designed to do—that is, to
add to knowledge by eliminating the mystery, by delv-
ing underneath the visible phenomena to discover the
why's and wherefore's of beautiful words or effective
people in order to learn what it is that differentiates
them from other phrases or actions. Unless we go
beyond the mysterious raptures of human behavior,
we can never truly know other people or understand
their values. Nor can we function effectively in writing
novels, operating a beauty salon, or gaining insight
into race relations or committee operations or the
peculiarities of relatives—or, finally, ourselves.

Benefits aside, the understanding of oneself and

one's society may be considered a moral and civic obligation of an educated man. Physical fitness enthusiasts, such as the late President Kennedy, have expressed the opinion that it is every man's duty to himself and his country to keep in good physical condition, and Olympic chairman Avery Brundage deemed it sinful not to develop oneself to his fullest muscular potential. Educators often take the same line concerning mental development: the Protestant Ethic binds many academicians to the idea that everyone has a duty to cultivate maximally his thinking prowess. Additionally, the investment by other persons of time and money in the intellectual maturation of a youth carries return obligations; as Jacques Barzun has pointed out, a college education is "a privilege the acceptance of which binds the taker" to look squarely at the social world. Grayson Kirk seconded this belief: "It is the responsibility of the educated man to make every effort, honestly and objectively, not only to understand the nature and problems of our society, but to comprehend compassionately the differences that separate it from others."[31] In 1884 Oliver Wendell Holmes Jr. expressed the same spirit plus an admixture of Socrates: "As life is action and passion, it is required of a man that he should share the passion and action of his time, at the peril of being judged not to have lived."

Two Sociologies

From this chapter's quick survey of basic sociological concepts and a small part of its vocabulary, one might infer correctly that the subject may be either quantitative or qualitative, scientific or verbal-philosophical, empirical or intuitive. Yet while sociology has acquired some of the attributes of all of these approaches, its direction in recent years has been toward the former of each dichotomy. The next five chapters discuss issues arising from the scientific character of sociology: social objectivity, securing and analyzing data, and mathematical and statistical operations. Chapter VII illustrates the application of such scientific methods to the study of social behavior.

But lest the other side of sociology be neglected to the extent that the discipline be portrayed as wholly scientific, it must be strongly emphasized that semi-scientific and nonscientific kinds of research and reasoning have also characterized sociology for many years. Presence of a scientific approach does not necessarily eliminate other approaches to the field; indeed, sociology has benefited greatly from nonscientific thinking and appears destined to continue doing so for some years to come.

It is regrettably true that while computing things, statisticians sometimes tend to treat people as numbers and to forget that each unit represents a living, feeling person. But this is not a sufficient reason to exclude quantification; rather, we should and do seek the advantages of both quantification and humane understanding, thus retaining the philosophical and humanistic elements present at the birth of sociology even as we add more and more scientific and statistical techniques. That such a beneficial coalition is feasible is demonstrated by the fact that statisticians still appreciate the fascination of music, the wonder of love, and the splendor of oceanside cliffs. Both the feasibility of this merger of scientific and nonscientific elements in a single individual and the tardiness of public acceptance of this possibility are evidenced by the awed facial expression accompanying a student's description of a sociology professor: "In class he keeps talking about scientific objectivity and measuring things, but deep down he's really a warm, loving person!"

Sociology is one area in which men can legitimately and successfully (though not always) combine the virtues of C. P. Snow's "two cultures" of science and humane learning. That Snow himself agrees is shown in the expanded version of his famous 1959 essay, in which the physicist-turned-novelist wrote hopefully of a rising "third culture" of social scientists.[32]

II

Sociology as a Science

∗

Contemporary sociologists are becoming increasingly oriented toward a scientific approach to their subject. The social philosophers who constituted a majority of sociologists at the opening of the twentieth century are now being outnumbered by the "new sociologists" trained in the methodology of scientific research. The somewhat premature system-building of early sociologists yielded in the first half of the century to the empiricism of men like George A. Lundberg and Samuel A. Stouffer. Objectors to this transition are inclined to view the shift as being one which has gone from a preponderance of architects and thinkers to a domination by bricklayers and laundry-ticket counters. Those pleased with this change contrast the "soft" facts of armchair theorizers with the "hard" facts of scientific data-gatherers. A scholar who understands both points of view has suggested a motto for the global theorists: "We do not know whether what we say is true, but it is at least significant." The radical empiricists reply: "We do not know whether what we say is significant, but it is at least true."[1]

The contrast between these antipodal positions can easily be overstressed; neither approach need be contradictory or antagonistic to the other. Indeed, some research combines the best elements of both. Precise observations may be rendered fascinating by their pertinence to timely and important issues. Questions for quantitative research may spring out of momentous conflicts. The untrained reader of a disciplined scientific research report may not recognize either its implications for social policy or its origins in speculative curiosity, but the connections frequently exist. Just as scientific research in physics may be associated with atomic warfare, so also scientific research in sociology may be connected with the violent storms of race relations. The results of social research are less magical in appearance than the electric sparks and whirling satellites of physics, but some are present and more are forthcoming from the relatively youthful science of sociology.

Perspective

To shift from global to personal matters, the major benefit to be derived from studying sociology is the sense of perspective that it gives us. It is frequently said that we cannot understand the present without knowledge of the past. But knowledge about our own past is not sufficient; one must also know something about other societies and their systems of belief, both past and present.

Wise sociologists thus avoid both ethnocentrism, the "view of things in which one's own group is the center of everything, and all others are scaled and rated with reference to it,"[2] and temporocentrism, "the unexamined and largely unconscious acceptance of one's own country, one's own era, one's own lifetime, as the center of sociological significance, as the focus to which all other periods of historical time are related, and as the criterion by which they are to be judged."[3]

Ethnocentric notions are world-wide, fostering jingoism and chauvinism. The opprobrious epithets "pig-eater," "cow-eater," "uncircumcised," "jabberer," and "frog" not only show contempt for the peculiarities of outsiders but also reinforce and intensify group cohesion.

> When Caribs were asked whence they came, they answered, "We alone are people." The meaning of the name Kiowa is "real or principal people." The Lapps call themselves "men" or "human beings." The Greenland Eskimos think that Europeans have been sent to Greenland to learn virtue and good manners from the Greenlanders. . . . The Jews . . . were the "chosen people." The Greeks and Romans called all outsiders "barbarians". . . . The Arabs regarded themselves as the noblest nation and all others as more or less barbarous. . . . Each state now regards itself as the leader of civilization, the best, the freest, and the wisest, and all others as inferior.[4]

Most people harbor the comforting and flattering delusion that their ways of doing things are the only sensible if not the only possible ones. If other peoples deviate from our practices they are thought of as amusingly quaint or dangerously bizarre; their eccentricities must be explained in the light of our preferred standards of behavior. Robert Lowie points out that the members of some groups do not accept our habits of eating three times a day or sleeping at night or driving on the right side of the road or pointing with the index finger. "There is only one way of finding out whether any particular idea or custom is natural or only conventional, to wit, experience; and that means not our limited experience in Ottumwa, Iowa, or the United States, or even in Western Civilization as a whole, but among all the peoples the world over."[5]

Still the world is wondrous large,—seven seas from
    marge to marge—
And it holds a vast of various kinds of man;

And the wildest dreams of Kew are the facts of Khat-
    mandhu,
And the crimes of Clapham chaste in Martaban.
Here's my wisdom for your use, as I learned it when
    the moose
    And the reindeer roamed where Paris roars to-
    night:—
"There are nine and sixty ways of constructing tribal
    lays,
    "And—every—single—one—of—them—is—right!"[6]

Kipling's metrical message is supported by cross-cul-
tural comparisons teaching that even supposedly instinctive motor habits like nodding the head, spitting,
crying, taking a present in the hand, and sticking out
the tongue have varying meanings determined by cultural definitions. Ethnologist Weston LaBarre supplies
examples of opposed meanings: "Western man stands
up in the presence of a superior; the Fijians and the
Tongans sit down. In some contexts we put on more
clothes as a sign of respect; the Friendly Islanders take
them off. The Toda of South India raise the open right
hand to the face, with the thumb on the bridge of the
nose, to express respect; a gesture almost identical
among Europeans is an obscene expression of extreme
disrespect."[7]

Ethical Neutrality

The same frame of mind that achieves perspective for
the student also supplies a foundation for the unbiased
objectivity of the research worker. If he wishes to be
called a scientist, a scholar must be neutral in the
performance of his research. Certainly he may and
does have opinions, but they cannot be allowed to influence his research operations.

Attitudes, of course, enter into everything that
people do—a fact of life that cannot help but affect
research. In choosing research subjects, both the physicist on his mountaintop and the behavioral scientist

use their opinions and beliefs to decide what is most interesting to them. So too with the financial sponsor: if he believes that too many people are dying, he may contribute money for antimortality research; if he is opposed to birth control, he will not donate money for this kind of research. These considerations also apply to the selection of the problem to be investigated. To be sure, scientists define science in such a way that this kind of value determination is permissible; but in the design, performance, and analysis of the study, neutrality is a *sine qua non.* To illustrate, a philanthropist supplies money to try to prevent juvenile delinquency. A sociologist decides that this subject interests him (perhaps because he wants to eliminate delinquency, perhaps because he is curious about its causes). Neither attitude is neutral. But when the sociologist does research to try to learn what causes delinquent behavior, he is obliged to design the project so that his disapproval of delinquency is irrelevant. In other words, even if he were in favor of increasing the delinquency rate, he would do the research in the same way. One of the major tasks of graduate schools is to train prospective sociologists to be objective. This skill does not come naturally or easily; it must be learned over a period of years of intensive directed work.

Sociological findings are frequently criticized on the basis that since no one can eliminate values from his thinking, social research perforce can never be truly scientific. Values are used in selecting a problem for study, because our values affect what interests us and what we think is the most useful direction for our activity. A physical scientist may make the value judgment that atomic research is more interesting than anything else; he also makes the judgment whether to do "pure" or "applied" research. It is virtually impossible to eliminate values from this stage of research. But once the subject is selected, the researcher must control his biases as completely as possible. First he must identify his values relevant to the subject, and then he must conduct the experiment so that these values cannot affect the results—that is, so that another investigator, holding different or opposite views, could perform the same experiment and arrive at identical results. The task of the social scientist is thus to recognize and allow for his biases during the study.

Simply because a man is studying the values of others does not mean that he is necessarily affected by his own values in the course of the study. Laymen often tend to confuse these two value influences. A man studying anti-Semitism need be neither anti-Semitic nor pro-Semitic. Lengthy training usually is required to enable the research worker to attain this level of perspective.

Discipline and Detachment

One reason why some laymen fail to understand sociology is that they cannot grasp the idea that anyone can impartially and objectively study human values. They doubt for example, that anyone can call a man a Negro as a statement of fact rather than as a personal attack, or apply the term "foreign born" descriptively rather than derogatively. Other laymen, thinking that values are fixed, divinely sanctioned, and therefore not subject to scientific scrutiny, condemn the sociologist as amoral or even immoral. Thus we return to the notion of sociological perspective; if people are too close to something or somebody, it is extremely difficult to see it as it really is. Unskilled observers let their emotions unduly intrude on and even define what they see; without considerable sociological knowledge and firm discipline, people can rarely maintain enough emotional detachment to understand fully their own society.

Most people take for granted the more familiar aspects of the social order, especially those features encountered at a very young age, which may come to be regarded as universal among mankind and an inevitable part of "human nature." Yet if we want to understand what makes our social world go around, we must study human behavior with the same detachment as does the chemist regarding a reaction in a test tube. The enthusiastic invention of innate tendencies and instincts is a case in point. At best it explains an unknown by postulating something still more unknown. Explaining war, for instance, as the outcome of the "combative instinct" simply postpones comprehension. Frequently too the elements of behavior that we call natural or instinctive are merely the folkways and mores to which we are habituated and with which we identify.

Instead of relying on instinct and other such superficial explanations, sociologists have developed a number of techniques enabling them to do research that can properly be called scientific. As expressed by Kingsley Davis: "Social behavior does not represent some special category of reality intrinsically impervious to systematic study. It is just as amenable to scientific investigation as any other natural phenomenon. The obstacles come, not from the subject matter itself, but from the limitations placed on the investigator by his own society."[8] Viscount Morley put it another way: "Where it is a duty to worship the sun, it is pretty sure to be a crime to examine the laws of heat."[9]

Resistance to Research

The latent and sometimes manifest popular hostility toward social science has been explained by Robert Merton: "Conflict arises when the social effects of applying scientific knowledge are deemed undesirable, when the scientist's skepticism is directed toward the basic values of other institutions, when the expansion of political or religious or economic authority limits the autonomy of the scientist, when anti-intellectualism questions the value and integrity of science and when non-scientific criteria of eligibility for scientific research are introduced."[10] Reasons for this opposition are not hard to find.

> A social system is always normative. Its integration rests upon the fact that its members carry in their heads, as part of the cultural heritage, the notion that they *ought* or *ought not* to do certain things, that some actions are *right* or *good* and others *wrong* or *bad*. Each person judges himself and his fellows according to these subtle and ubiquitous rules; and any violation is punished by some negative reaction, be it slight or great. An evaluative attitude, an attitude of praise and blame, of accusation and justification, thus pervades every human society. To question the rules, or worse yet, to question the sentiments lying behind them, is to incur certain penalties, the least of which is controversy. The person who tries in his own thinking to escape entirely the moralistic system in order to study behavior objectively, who tries to analyze social norms and values as if they were amoebae or atoms, is quickly branded as an agnostic, cynic, traitor, or worse. Instead of public support for his work, he must count on public hostility.[11]

The world-renowned zoologist Alfred C. Kinsey had no difficulty studying the wasp, but as soon as he focussed his microscope on human sexual behavior, he was in trouble. "There were attempts by the medical association in one city to bring suit on the ground that we were practicing medicine without a license, police interference in two or three cities, investigation by a sheriff in one rural area, and attempts to persuade the University's administration to stop the study, or to prevent the publication of the results, or to dismiss the senior author from his university connection, or to establish a censorship over all publications emanating from the study."[12]

The slowness of social science to gain wide public acceptance may be attributed to two circumstances. First, as social science scrutinizes traditional and existing institutions, practices, and values, it threatens the public with "dangerous" thoughts. Second, since social science problems appear to be the same as those of an ordinary citizen, the public thinks social science is simply common sense confused by erudite verbiage.[13]

The traditional stereotype of social behavior as immune to scientific experimentation is analogous to the now obsolete fight concerning biological science. Georges Cuvier, the founder of comparative anatomy, believed that physiology could never become an inductive science: "All parts of a living body are interrelated; they can act only in so far as they act all together; trying to separate one from the whole means transferring it to the realm of dead substances; it means entirely changing its essence."[14] In reply, the great physiologist Claude Bernard offered splendid testimony to scientific method in refuting this claim: "The spontaneity enjoyed by beings endowed with life has been one of the principal objections urged against the use of experimentation in biological studies. . . . The science of vital phenomena must have the same foundations as the science of the phenomena of inorganic bodies, and . . . there is no difference in this respect between the principles of biological science and those of physico-chemical science."[15] To which now should be added: the same for social science.

Feasibility of Social Science

Arguments that human behavior is inherently resistant to scientific analysis (whereas inanimate movement and animal behavior are easily measured and analyzed) are misleading—indeed, spurious. We can and do measure how people act and record what they say. Not only is it easier to take a census of the number of people in a town than to count the number of fish in a lake, the number of deer in a forest, the number of rabbits in a field, or the number of birds in the sky, but the results are far more accurate. Human fertility, mortality, and migration are all better recorded than

comparable animal behavior. Investigators do a better
job of ascertaining the ages of large groups of humans
than of leopards, sharks, pelicans, or penguins.

Laymen sometimes contend that people are very
easy to understand (hence, social science is unnecessary)—or very difficult to understand (hence, social
science is impossible). Sociologists correctly respond
that we are doing our job as well as most other scientists are doing theirs.

Sociologists at times express envy of the physicists'
presumed superior ability to manipulate and measure
the phenomena of their field; physicists often retort
that where accuracy is concerned, "things are tough
all over," and that social science is not so far behind
physical science as one might believe—and probably
on a par with biological science. Consider for instance
how often the chemistry professor's test tube lecture
demonstration fails to work—or note the Princeton as-
tronomer's remark to a sociologist that "your data are
more accurate than ours." The popular fancy that
scientists can establish perfect experimental control
and secure unqualifiedly accurate data is fallacious;
hence the necessary resort to statistical reporting and
probabilistic explanation in all scientific fields. And
where statistical techniques are concerned, sociology
appears as well equipped as any other discipline.

Human Predictability

Many laymen claim that the behavior of human
beings is unpredictable. But the existence of scientific
sociology is based on the assumption that human behavior is consistent, amenable to generalizations, and
predictable. Accordingly, we change the layman's
question: "Are our actions predictable?" to "What information is needed to predict?" Indeed, human beings
are highly consistent in their actions; we are unaware
of the extent of this consistency because we take it for
granted, noticing only the deviations. Take a fairly

prosaic example: driving. We bet our lives on other drivers' predictability every time we set out in our cars. While driving, we complain about other drivers who do the unexpected; yet if we count cars, we discover that actually a very small minority act unexpectedly. Even at that, most so-called driving irregularities are a function of our own ignorance or inattention—the driver who slows suddenly and evokes our wrath may be reacting to a pedestrian or a "parking place" occupied by an "invisible" Volkswagen. The next time you drive on a highway, reflect on how much confidence you are perforce placing (despite your vigorous protestations to the contrary) on the driver directly in front of you.

Where conditions of reward and punishment are clear, human behavior is extremely predictable. When a police car is visible, what proportion of the people drive through a red light? When employees are fired or docked for absence, we can predict rather well the number of absentees in a large plant in the month of October—especially if the weather forecasts are accurate. (Compare attendance prediction with weather prediction.) Finally, consider the student leaving his fraternity house for a 10:00 class; professors who know the current clothing fads (tennis shoes, saddle shoes, sandals, and the like) can make excellent predictions about the student's attire. Social life would be impossible without some degree of predictability—or conformity.

Surprisingly, human behavior appears upon close inspection to be about as predictable as are physical phenomena in comparable situations. In the real world (as contrasted with the carefully contrived situations of the laboratory), physical scientists are not universally successful. New machines developed by trained physicists and engineers always have "bugs" needing to be eradicated; the "bugs" in a new automobile engine are essentially physical predictions that have gone wrong. Even given the vast budgets and superlative material and technical resources of space missile and satellite research, mistakes are frequent. In the case of the first United States manned space flight, malfunction of physical equipment had to be compensated for by a properly functioning human being in order to achieve a reasonably successful landing. When an airplane flight or train trip is delayed, the fault is more likely to be mechanical than human—though it must be admitted that there may be more physical than human components involved. Natural scientists know they cannot predict next year's epidemics, floods, mountain slides, and earthquakes. All this being so, why then should criminologists be ashamed of their record of prediction in parole cases? It would seem that accurate forecasting is no more the property of physics than of sociology.[16]

Determinism and Probability

Modern science is infused with probabilistic reasoning. Sir Arthur Stanley Eddington has remarked: "It is impossible to trap modern physics into predicting anything with perfect determinism because it deals with probabilities from the outset." Atomic physicist Max Born wrote: "The conception of chance enters into the very first steps of scientific activity. . . . I think chance is a more fundamental conception than causality; for whether in a concrete case a cause-effect relation holds or not can only be judged by applying the laws of chance to the observations." Nobel Prize physicist Werner Heisenberg, explaining his new nonlinear spinor theory of elementary particles, stressed the idea that "the world of the atom is one of probability, rather than certainty." Both natural and social scientists tend to adopt a probabilistic approach to description and prediction in recognition of the absurdity of assuming invariability of phenomena.

Thus the obsolescent argument between free will and determinism is yielding place to a modified determinist view based on probability. In fact, probability is invading field after field of man's knowledge. Life insurance companies are among the world's richest corporations in part because they can predict so well the proportion of their policy-holders who will die in each coming year. Others who couch their findings and opinions in probabilistic terms include psychologists, economists, chemists, and philosophers. We may soon reach the point where the elements of inductive statistics, which is founded on probability, will be recognized as so necessary to all educated men to be required for college graduation just as freshman English is required today. Even practitioners of "the art of healing" now think and talk of the probability of patients surviving a given ailment or operation, based on previous experience with similar patients.

The fact of the matter is that unless we accept some version of determinism, science is simply not workable. If everyone always acted of his own free will, generalizations would be impossible and predictions fruitless. Sociology as a scientific approach to human behavior is founded on an assumption that some form of determinism accurately portrays human beliefs and actions.

A deterministic system is one in which the properties at any given time are a function of its properties at previous times.[17] For example, how persons vote in the next Presidential election will be a function of their previous voting record, educational level, parents' political affiliations, and so forth. Yet, while these previous properties have an obvious bearing on the coming vote, it is extremely difficult in our present state of knowledge to ascertain the precise degree of influence of each factor. Still, many people believe that they can predict the outcome of the next election, whether they admit to using deterministic reasoning or not.

Hypotheses and Variables

Sociological research explores the relationships between two or more attributes or actions—for example, the relationship between a man's political affiliation and his father's. Sociologists want to know the kind and extent of the connections between social events. Efforts to understand and eventually to predict belief and behavior profit by use of hypotheses, experimental design, theories, and analysis of causation.

Interrelationships are expressed as questions or as hypotheses—in serious research they are usually stated as hypotheses. An hypothesis is a statement concerning the interplay between two factors or variables. It is "a proposition, condition, or principle which is assumed, perhaps without belief, in order to draw out its logical consequences and by this method to test its accord with facts which are known or may be determined."[18] It may be addressed to cause (as in "A is the cause of B") or to statistical correlation (as in "A is associated with B").

Null hypotheses, which lend themselves particularly well to testing, are statements of no difference or no relationship. For example, we might set up the null hypothesis that there is no difference in income between college graduates and noncollege graduates; or that migrants have the same intelligence level as nonmigrants. A statistical significance test would then be applied, resulting in either acceptance or rejection of the hypothesis.

The word "variable," often used by sociologists, refers to "any trait, quality, or characteristic which can vary in magnitude in different individual cases."[19] In testing an hypothesis concerning the relationship between two variables, one variable is called dependent, the other independent. The dependent variable may follow or be influenced by its independent counterpart. Frequently there are several independent variables potentially affecting the dependent variable. For instance, if the dependent variable is the decision whether or not to have more children, some possible independent variables might include number of children already in the family, religion, age of parents, income, education, size of community of residence, and sense of security.

According to the empiricists, "hard" knowledge is obtained through formulating and testing hypotheses concerning the relation between dependent and independent variables. To identify the relevant variables, a scholar must be well read in the literature of his subject. As Louis Pasteur said, "In the field of observation, chance favors only the prepared mind." Empirical research requires both methodological competence and a scholarly knowledge of the subject matter.

The Controlled Experiment

Rigorous social and physical scientists define "science" in terms of the methods used to acquire knowledge. Specifically, if experimental controls are used whenever appropriate, the research is designated as scientific.

The essence of the controlled experiment is that two groups differing only in one relevant respect are studied. One group (the experimental group) is subjected to the stimulus under test, while the other (the control group) is not. By taking measurements of each group both before and after the administration of the experimental stimulus, scientists are able to make sound inferences about the cause-effect relationship they are investigating. For example, suppose we are studying anti-Russian attitudes among Americans. Having divided the Americans into an experimental and a control group, we must first match the two groups to ensure that both have identical (or at least very similar) attitudes toward Russia initially. Then we show the experimental group a movie extolling the merits of the American way of life and derogating the Russians.

Lest the findings be invalidated, the experimental and control groups are kept apart. Finally both groups are tested regarding their attitudes toward Russia. If the experiment has been carried out according to the rather strict dictates of scientific accuracy, we may attribute to the effect of the movie any changes in attitude among members of the experimental group (insofar as they differ from comparable changes that may occur in the control group). This process of matching, premeasuring the effect, exposing to the stimulus, measuring the results, and analyzing the influence of the movie is in practice far more sophisticated and complicated than has been described here, but essentially the procedure is as delineated.

Sociological research more and more tends to follow this type of procedure. To be sure, it is often difficult and sometimes impractical to perform a "pure" or "natural" experiment involving social phenomena, but sociologists have developed a number of methodological techniques (for instance, the *ex post facto* experiment described in Chapter IV) to do research which satisfies the canons of scientific rigor.[20]

The Role of Theory

The primary task of science is to isolate principles of as general validity as possible. For example, the actions of freely falling bodies anywhere on earth are accounted for by the formula: $s = v_0 t + \frac{1}{2}gt^2$, where s is distance traveled, v_0 is initial velocity, t is time, and g is acceleration due to gravity. (The variables v_0 and t differ with each situation; the parameter g remains constant for any given location but takes on different values at different places.) Theory is indispensable in this task. Without a theoretical framework to bind the facts together, knowledge would be fragmented into a collection of discrete segments of unconnected statements. With a theory, these facts are made far more meaningful, allowing the scientist to construct more and more inclusive generalizations and laws. Empirical facts are explained by low level generalizations, which in turn are explained by Merton's "theories of the middle range," which then are pulled together by a higher order theory on a still higher level of abstraction.[21]

This steady progress of science toward more and more inclusive laws and principles may be called the pyramidal tendency of scientific theorizing. To illustrate, Kepler's three laws of planetary motion and Galileo's laws concerning freely falling bodies were combined into Newton's universal law of gravitation. Oersted's experiments with magnetism and Faraday's work in electricity were put together by Clerk-Maxwell to form his electromagnetic field theory. In turn, these two generalizations—the first concerning gravitation, the second concerning electromagnetism—formed the bases for Einstein's theory of relativity, which was developed from the theoretical knowledge contributed by Newton and Clerk-Maxwell. Thus we have a pyramid constructed of an upper theory, two middle theories, and four sets of empirical generalizations.

The pyramidal tendency plays a major part in the success of scientists in explaining and predicting physical and social phenomena. Evidence for propositions in systems accumulates much faster than for independent propositions, since in the former case both direct and indirect verification and refutation are possible. Furthermore, several hypotheses may be tested simultaneously when they form part of a theoretical structure. And finally, research performed without the guidance of theory is usually sterile for the reason that the investigator does not know quite what data to look for—and, when he has them, he cannot put them to use.[22]

Theoretical Explanation

The number of unconnected elements in a theoretical system is kept to a minimum following the dictates of the principle of parsimony. Fourteenth-century English philosopher William of Occam said: "No more causes are to be assumed than are necessary to account for the phenomena." This rule, known as Occam's razor, cuts off much unnecessary superstructure. In the words of Albert Einstein, "the grand aim of all science . . . is to cover the greatest possible number of empirical facts by logical deduction from the smallest possible number of hypotheses or axioms. Meanwhile the train of thought leading from the axioms to the empirical facts or verifiable consequences gets steadily longer and more subtle."[23] In modern sociology functional analysis has the objective of finding a set of properties or variables such that the specific forms of all the properties of a system are "uniquely determined by these n properties at that time, and such that n is the smallest number of properties for which this holds."[24]

Systematic interconnecting of facts is the object of science; unrelated facts are a challenge to the scientific mind. A fact as such has very little meaning; but when it is placed into systematic or theoretical relationship to other facts, meaning is created.

The classical view of Aristotle, Bacon, and Newton that a set of facts uniquely determines a theory is no longer tenable. As J. H. Poincaré claimed, any phenomenon which can be explained by one theory can also be explained by any number of other theories. In this regard scientists have sometimes posited several hypotheses to explain a given set of data—for instance, the wave and corpuscular theories of light and the various competing theories of the origin of the solar system.

Confronting a set of facts about the solar system or the social system, the physical or social scientist, faced with many possible such avenues of theorizing, explores the one that seems to offer the fullest explanation in the fewest terms. But whatever mode of explanation the theorist advances, the inception of a theory stems from a combination of three essential ingredients: knowledge of established facts, logical analyses of these facts' manifest interconnections, and above all, inventiveness in surmising the latent relations of such evidence to underlying physical or social forces or propensities. In short, a theory results from an imaginative leap, whether it occurs while its author is working in the laboratory or smoking in bed or stepping out of a bus. This indispensability of imagination is part of what Albert Einstein argued in writing of the value of imagination in scientific achievement. Claude Bernard also stressed the essential parts played by the initial idea or hypothesis and the subsequent idea clarifying the observed phenomena.[25]

Social Causation

A major objective of science is to identify and dissect causal connections between independent and dependent variables. To this end, we set up hypotheses relating two or more variables and then test the hypotheses for verification or refutation, employing a battery of statistical and methodological techniques. Underlying these research operations are theoretical propositions regarding functional relations and the nature of social causation.[26]

Social theorists seek to understand the reasons why people act and think as they do. To achieve this goal, theorists try out a considerable number of independent variables, each of which has some prospect of explaining changes in the dependent variable.

Some theories are highly complex, involving many variables; others attempt to explain human behavior in terms of one factor. These single-factor theories are often incomplete and have been labelled "particularistic fallacies" because of their tendency toward a unitary explanation of complex phenomena. At its worst, particularism may take the form of Marxian emphasis on the class struggle, neo-Freudian infant sexuality, or

Huntington's overstress of the influence of climate on the level of civilization. Nonetheless, single-factor theories must not be disregarded. Originators of theories often overemphasize one causative variable simply because it has heretofore been ignored. Moreover, the cumulative effect of these theories may be considerable. As has been noted: "The history of social theory is largely a series of statements asserting that some one factor is the sole cause of social change."[27]

The search for causes is thus bound up both with Einstein's imaginative leap inspiring a theory and with Edison's "99 per cent perspiration" in testing the theory against "the cruel facts." Two elements essential to verification are the collection of observed data and their subsequent analysis, which form the substance of the following two chapters.

III

Collecting Information

＊

Social research has as its primary goal the understanding of social life by discovering new facts, documenting or rejecting old ones, tracing sequences and connections between events, and formulating generalizations concerning interrelationships. In seeking to satisfy human curiosity through adding to knowledge (rather than "doing good" by manipulating people's lives), social scientists usually proceed through an approximation to the following series of steps.

Steps in Doing Social Research

1. *Selection of an interesting topic*—and perhaps, though not necessarily, a significant or useful one. The topic may be suggested by a theory, an apparent conflict between two theories, a gap in knowledge, or some other combination of inquisitiveness, creative hunches, and proficiency in the subject.

2. *Formulation of working hypotheses.* The translation of an interesting but quasi-specific question into an objectively testable hypothesis demands far more

skill than might be supposed by the novice. This conversion of an interesting problem into researchable form is prerequisite to the determination of exactly what information will be relevant.

3. *Deciding on the manner of securing data.* This decision is generally restricted by decisions made in steps 1 and 2—and in practice the experienced researcher makes allowance for step 3 when formulating his hypotheses. The many available methods of securing such data are outlined in this chapter.

4. *Collection of relevant data.* This operation constitutes the actual performance of the study (the interviewing, for example), as opposed to the anticipatory nature of the first three steps. Sometimes suitable data are already available (the wise researcher always considers this possibility in contemplating steps 2 and 3), in which event, collection consists of copying.

5. *Analysis of the data by statistical and other techniques.* By computing percentages, averages, and more sophisticated measures, the investigator facilitates comprehension of what otherwise might be simply a chaotic mass of information too vast and complicated to be grasped by inspection.

6. *Interpretation of results.* Comparing the theory of step 1 and the hypotheses of step 2 with the findings of steps 4 and 5 has the objective of accepting or rejecting hypotheses and perhaps the theories or laws from which they were deduced. New generalizations may be advanced for later testing.

7. *Presentation of findings and conclusions.* Though the research proper is completed with step 6, publication or other announcement of the results is desirable and customary. Otherwise the work is likely to be wasted.

8. *Application of results.* For maximum value of the research project, many sponsors prefer to see the results incorporated into an action program. It is this practical application that justifies the research to the public by making possible a faster rocket or a better

mousetrap. The pure researcher, of course, is expected to disdain crass practicality in the tradition of certain ancient Athenians.

Design, Performance, Analysis, and Use

These eight intertwined steps form four phases. Steps 1 through 3 constitute the design or "before" segment of the research operation. Since all subsequent steps depend on them, their importance cannot be overemphasized. It is during the design phase that most studies are made or broken. The astute researcher anticipates later steps in considerable detail while elaborating the design of his study. Inexperienced investigators generally try to proceed too quickly to phase two. A reasonable though incomplete basis for distinguishing quickly between competent and incompetent research workers is that the latter are rarely sufficiently disciplined to think through the consequences for steps 4, 5, and 6 of the decisions they make so enthusiastically in steps 1 through 3.

Step 4, the performance or "during" stage, is also essential to the study, though far less critical intellectually than steps 1 through 3. Since lower levels of skills are demanded here than in the design phase, and since more routine "leg work" is required, this part of the project is often entrusted to hired helpers lacking the intelligence, training, or experience of the director. Obviously, the work must be well done or the findings will be valueless, but it is not inappropriate that work done during step 4 be rewarded at a lower rate of pay than the decision-making of steps 1-3. Experience in the interviewing and clerical operations of this second phase is normally prerequisite to becoming a research director or intellectual entrepreneur.

There are two "after" phases. Steps 5 and 6 constitute the final part of the research work proper, when the investigator combines the ideas and tabulations into a meaningful whole. This phase is almost as critical as the design, though if steps 2 and 3 have been well conceived, the data analysis often proceeds fairly smoothly and easily; however, unexpected findings often pose—or impose—more problems than they solve. Exposition of this phase forms the backbone of the next chapter.

The second "after" phase—steps 7 and 8—though not a part of formal research, is frequently incorporated into the research process through assignment of money to support publication or through inclusion of action-orientation in step 1 and occasionally in step 2. Different skills are required here than are requisite in steps 1 through 6; not only are many researchers unable to write fluently or even clearly, but most seem uninterested or ineffectual in "selling" their conclusions to someone with enough power to enact legislation or otherwise seek to alter human actions.

This chapter will consider steps 3 and 4—the gathering of data; other phases will be discussed in following chapters. What the reader would do well to remember in connection with this chapter is that whether information is copied from existing records (secondary use of data) or painstakingly acquired by interviewing or observing (primary data), the researcher is not bound to restrict himself to a single source or method. Most of the techniques in this and the following chapter are mutually compatible and can be used to supplement each other. In fact, many sociological studies employ several of these techniques.

Documentary Material

The performance phase of a sociological study may be carried out either by collecting one's own data or making use of data that someone else has already collected. Such pre-existing data may be secured from a variety of sources, both qualitative and quantitative: archives, censuses, professional journals, diaries, biographies, histories, films, literature, and many others.

The investigator often elects to use such existing material because it saves the considerable time and expense that would be lost if he collected the data himself.

In other cases the researcher has no choice because he is unable to obtain the data himself. When a study involving social change dictates use of factual material covering a lengthy time span, historical documents must be consulted. When different cultures are to be studied, it is often financially or otherwise impossible for the researcher to visit the other societies, especially if they are numerous. When complete coverage on a national or metropolitan scale is demanded, government sources (such as the United States census) must be consulted because only the government has the resources adequate to such large-scale enumeration. Inaccessibility stems also from a variety of other circumstances: business corporations, social organizations, and government agencies often restrict access to their official records or informal meetings, thus compelling the social scientist to accept whatever material is distributed by the group instead of going directly to the records themselves or actually attending meetings.

Uses of documents are many. Census statistics state the number and characteristics of the people of, say, West Virginia in 1910 as compared with 1960. School curricula of 1890 are compared with 1924 curricula as an indication of changing views concerning what the adults of a community think it important for their children to know.[1] The tendency of pre-Civil War newspaper advertisements to sell Negro slave mothers and their children under age 10 as a unit (whereas fathers were much less frequently sold together with their children) was taken by Frazier as evidence that the slave family was primarily matriarchal.[2] Burial inscriptions from ancient cemeteries supply partial evidence concerning ages at death in those times.[3] The plays of Aristophanes and Euripides are a major source of knowledge and speculation concerning the role of

women in Greek life.[4] Freud even tried to psycho-
analyze Leonardo da Vinci from a distance of four
centuries.[5]

Observational Methods

Somewhat less susceptible to attack on grounds of
inaccuracy are those procedures in which the investigator himself—or his hirelings—sees and records the
events under examination. Observational techniques
fall into three categories: participant observation, systematic field observation, and laboratory observation.

Participant observation, as the name implies, is distinguished by the fact that the observer himself forms
a part of the group or situation he is studying. He ex-
amines street corner gangs by joining one;[6] he investigates dance band musicians by playing in a band.[7]
The rather obvious weakness of this procedure—that
the persons being observed may be influenced by the
presence of the observer—is supplemented by the less
apparent but also undesirable possibility that the observer, though participating, identifies so much with
the group that he may lose his own objectivity. Participant observation is particularly suited to studying
groups about which so little is known that more systematic procedures cannot yet be applied.

Systematic observation of field situations consists
essentially of watching but not participating in the
events under study.[8] This everyday outlet for curiosity
(as in watching crowds at parades or noting leadership in informal childrens' games) is systematized and
transformed into a research tool by careful notation
of time, personnel, regularities, deviations, incentives,
cohesiveness, goal directions, and so forth—whatever
variables are relevant to testing the hypotheses derived
from the theoretical stance engendering the research.
Usually the situation is totally independent of the investigator's influence: events arise, groups form and
dissolve, fights break out, and jobs are done whether

he is present or not. Yet this circumstance itself limits use of field observation; for instance, someone studying rioting has to wait for a riot to occur—and then hope to be able to reach the scene before the rioters disperse.

If it is desirable to confront the subjects with specified situations, laboratory observation is adopted.[9] This methodologically more sophisticated technique may be used in a room with a one-way screen from which the researcher can observe but remain unobserved himself. The subjects, for instance, may play a card game with the deck stacked in such manner that players are presented with certain standardized decisions (for example, to play "close to the vest" or "Devil take the hindmost"). Or a small group of people may be asked to decide which of two lines is longer, the first few persons being shills or stooges instructed to state that the shorter line looks longer to them; the experimenter then observes the extent of influence of these palpably incorrect statements on the subsequently expressed opinions of the other members of the group.[10]

Irrespective of which technique is used, the observational nexus should not introduce distortions. This is the reason for concealing the investigator—or at least his purpose. Since subject awareness of the observer's presence or the fact of experimentation may distort response, some investigators thus confine their observation to spontaneous events—or try to simulate the freshness of day-to-day experience. The contrived situations of the laboratory are dangerous to accuracy; if the situation seems artificial to them, subjects may behave abnormally.

Projective Techniques

As in the case of laboratory observation, projective techniques generally were developed by psychologists and are used more often in psychology than in sociology. Projective tests evoke verbal or other reactions from which inferences may be drawn concerning the subject's values and attitudes. Their distinguishing property is that the true purpose is disguised. But while their customary use is therapeutic, they are also useful as research tools.

Free association methods modified from Carl Jung's word association (familiar to everyone through extensive use in party games) are sentence completion and story completion. In Murray's Thematic Apperception Test, subjects are requested to tell a story about each of a series of ambiguous pictures; each person presumably reads into the pictures the values, attitudes, hopes, and fears that dominate—manifestly and latently—his thoughts, perceptions, and aspirations. Hermann Rorschach's famous ink blot charts have been used since 1911 to elicit unguarded and presumably revealing interpretations. Responses to both the T.A.T. and Rorschach tests are analyzed for certain themes: quantity of response, originality, active or static quality, human-animal-inanimate preferences, positiveness, self-identification, and the like. Psychodrama and play techniques require subjects to act out roles in real-life situations (the office wife) or to manipulate playthings (white and colored dolls). Disguised attitude tests are also employed: information questions having all wrong or indeterminable answers, reasoning tests in which personal opinion may affect the syllogistic inference, requests for other people's opinions as clues to the subject's own opinion, and tests of perception or memory influenced by idiosyncratic predispositions.

Questionnaires and Schedules

Sociologists usually rely on more direct procedures calling for less intuitive interpretation, notably the interview and the self-administering questionnaire; the former is distinguished by the presence of an interviewer who reads or adapts questions from an interview schedule, whereas in the latter case questionnaires

are distributed and collected by mail or administered
to large groups by a non-interviewing supervisor.
These two techniques have the additional advantage
of lending themselves to quantification.

This is not to say that interviews and questionnaires
are only valuable for quantitative social research.
Quite the contrary; the classic qualitative case study
is founded on intensive informal interrogation and discussion. Whether the motive be amelioration of ills or
discovery of facts, the social worker's interview and
the scientific research questionnaire have the common
quality of placing reliance on the respondent's verbal
reporting of unobserved feelings and experiences.
Viewed in this light, these verbal techniques are sub-
stitutes for observational methods, which are frequently impractical and usually less efficient in ex-
pending the researcher's time and money.

In order to elicit accurate oral or written accounts
of the respondents' beliefs and actions, interview
schedules and self-administered questionnaires must
be constructed with extreme care. First, however, the
researcher must decide just what data are really
needed to test his hypotheses. Amateurs have a tendency to collect too much information, often adopting
the easy route of including all questions that "might
yield something interesting." Questionnaires must be
held down to a reasonable length, which forces omission of some pet questions. Some experienced men
recommend preparing dummy tables or table shells—
tables having headings across the top and along the
side, but no figures in the rows and columns—as a
means of focusing attention on specific item-by-item
comparisons; if a question does not appear useful in a
dummy table, it is omitted.

Aside from information identifying the interviewer
and respondent, two types of items are included in
schedules. First, background or census-type data are
used to describe the respondents in the fundamental
terms relevant to most sociological issues: age, sex,

birthplace, marital status, education, religion, occupation and so forth. The bulk of the schedule, however, is made up of questions relating to the subject of the study. Inclusion of some items is dictated by the hypotheses: thus if a hypothesis states that A is associated with B, then both A and B must be included in order to ascertain the truth of the hypothesis.

Questions vary in spirit, style, and provision for response: invariable or flexible phrasing; check response, short answer, or free (open end) response; a single question or series of questions on a point; direct or indirect approach; structured (for example, "what TV program are you watching now?") or unstructured ("what do you think of TV?"); or personal or impersonal orientation. Ordering of questions is important. They should carry the respondent through the interview effortlessly, arouse interest, avoid resistance, and not unduly bias subsequent questions. Content and phrasing should be consistent with the respondent's education, vocabulary, and experience.

In view of the demands set by these and other considerations, usually interview schedules not surprisingly go through several drafts before reaching their final versions. Sociologists generally pretest schedules —that is, try them out by administering them to a small but representative sample. Pretesting results in rewording, dropping questions, adding others, changing question sequence—and then, time permitting, doing another pretest. Questionnaires and schedules are beset by the same semantic and rhetorical difficulties of any communication cutting across ethnic, class, and other boundaries. When both northerners and southerners or both farmers and metropolitanites are to be interviewed in one study, the investigator must be careful of his use of, say, "evening" (variously defined as after 12 noon, after 6 P.M., and after 9 P.M.), "visit" (meaning informal neighboring or formal occasions), "dinner" (eaten at noon, 5 P.M., 7 P.M., or 10 P.M.—and at a different hour on Sunday), and numerous other innocuous-appearing terms that may hinder insight or cloak misunderstanding in apparent comprehension.

Interviewing

The possibility of misunderstanding does not end with discovering an approximately optimum wording and sequence of questions. Interviewers must also ask the questions in such a way that respondents will answer honestly and fully. To this end, interviewers must establish rapport or harmonious relations with the respondent. But while there are many rules for achieving and maintaining rapport (do not rush respondents, be a good listener, and so forth), a large school of thought favors the position that good interviewers are born, not taught. Certainly a skilled questioner needs ample supplies of personality, training, and experience.

There are three kinds of interviews: poll-type, informal, and analytical. The poll-type interviewer reads questions precisely as they are written and otherwise adheres exactly to instructions. Little skill is demanded. The second type of interview, variously known as the informal, intensive, qualitative, conversational, or case history interview, allows the interviewer moderate latitude. He may select any one of several phrasings of a question, or he may change the order of questions if the respondent leads him unexpectedly to a topic that normally appears later in the interview. Using the interview schedule as a guide to be adapted individually to each respondent, he is thus able to follow up clues to the respondent's perceptive set or orientation. Analytical interviewing, which permits almost unlimited latitude, falls in the domain of the psychiatrist, psychoanalyst, or psychiatric social worker. Since it is rarely used for research purposes and requires extensive training, it is beyond the scope of this book.

Let us contrast the three interview types with an example. Questioning respondents as regards their reading habits, the poll-type interviewer might ask "What is your favorite magazine?" (answer: *Time*); the informal interviewer would ask the further question "Why do you prefer *Time?*" (answer arrived at indirectly: "because it gives the reader a feeling of being a busy executive"); and the analytical interviewer would try to ascertain why the respondent needs to feel like a busy executive.

Informal interviews contain probes, that is, follow-up questions designed to elaborate, clarify, qualify, contradict, or otherwise shed light on a response just given. Following an answer to the classic question: "Have you stopped beating your wife?", an interviewer would add the classic probe, "Why?" If the respondent describes himself, say, as an engineer, a probe is called for to determine the sense in which the word is being used—does he design rockets, drive a locomotive, or perform duties once designated by the title "janitor"? Probes have several purposes: to resolve apparent or actual inconsistencies of replies, to direct the respondent to a certain aspect of response, to explain a misunderstood question, or to encourage amplification of replies. Shrewd use of probes may transform routine questioning which elicits superficial replies into penetrating questioning which evokes deeply-felt hidden responses.

Astute probing requires understanding of the dimensions of response to an item. To the question, "Why did you buy Brand X?", the respondent may state that she likes the taste, that her favorite supermarket carries it, or that she always buys it. The three dimensions involved are, in order: attributes of the product (taste, appearance, healthfulness); influences on the buyer (her supermarket, friend's recommendation, newspaper advertisement); and attitude of the buyer toward the product (fondness, hatred, indifference). The question as phrased leaves to the respondent the choice of dimension. Sometimes this unstructured context is what the researcher wants, but at other times he is supposed to probe for one particular dimension—or to continue probing until all three dimensions are covered. Alternatively, in a poll-type interview, the question may be recast to direct the respondent toward a certain dimension: "What do you like best about Brand X?" (attribute); "Who first suggested you buy Brand X?" (influence); "Have you ever considered buying another brand?" (attitude).

Whether poll-type or intensive, the interview's content and direction are determined by the hypotheses under examination. Probes and careful phrasings serve the purpose of directing the respondent's reply to the dimension of response demanded by each hypothesis.

Sampling versus Enumeration

Since question design, interviewing, tabulation of responses, and statistical analysis all are both time-consuming and expensive, social scientists frequently sample rather than conduct a complete enumeration. Taking samples introduces risks, but they are compensated for by several advantages, of which greater speed and less expense are only two. Given fixed resources, an investigator may use a sample in preference to complete enumeration in order to devote more attention to the details of each case—he may elect to examine 300 cases intensively instead of 300,000 cases superficially. The greater attention devoted to each return often results in superior accuracy and more variables being included in the study. Frequently sampling permits hiring more highly trained personnel; for instance, the United States census in recent decades has required about 150,000 interviewers—but there are not 150,000 skilled interviewers in the country. Hence data concerning sensitive subjects such as income and sexual relations may be secured more accurately by using a small sample and highly competent interviewers.

On the other hand, sampling does have its faults.

Sampling variability can never be eliminated (though it can be measured through statistical operations described in Chapter V). Sample studies are also generally harder to design than complete enumerations. Finally, sampling is sometimes impractical, as where the sought-after characteristic is extremely rare or where a highly convoluted design would be needed.

There are situations in which researchers are compelled to sample. Some populations are infinite and could never be studied completely (all possible human families). Some populations are finite but vast (the people of the world). Others are so inaccessible that complete enumeration is impractical (all living graduates of the University of California—many of whom have left no forwarding addresses). Experimental control may demand a sample (if everyone receives a given stimulus, who is left to be in the control group?). Finally, if sociologists attempted to administer every public opinion questionnaire to everyone in the nation, the time spent in answering questions would prove an intolerable burden to the populace.

Judgment and Probability Sampling

There are two broad types of sampling—judgment and probability—each of which is subdivided into subtypes. Judgment samples, in which respondents are selected at the discretion of the interviewers or their supervisors, are generally inferior to probability samples, which are independent of the predilections and impulses of the investigators.

The distinguishing attribute of judgment samples is that the sample members are chosen selectively, thus introducing conscious or unconscious judgment on the part of the person making the selection. In this method of choosing sample members, bias is inevitable. Two subtypes of judgment sampling are quota and purposive samples. In quota sampling, the population is classified by pertinent attributes, and each interviewer is assigned a quota from each class. But while this procedure is inexpensive, its accuracy is so low as to prohibit its use in serious research. In purposive sampling, members are carefully picked out as typical or as forming barometer groups—for example, "As Maine goes, so goes the Nation." This technique is best characterized as "hopeless."[11]

Probability samples are designed so that sample members are chosen automatically, with no judgment on the part of the person doing the drawing. They offer the advantage of knowing the likelihood that any person in the universe or total population will be included in the sample—an exceedingly valuable property, since it permits application of statistical and mathematical formulas for the calculation of error. By contrast, we cannot compute sampling errors for judgment samples. Correctly designed probability samples eliminate personal bias (as in choosing on the basis of convenience or opinion). As an example, if the president of a denominational college wishes to ascertain student opinion about installing billiard tables in the student union, he might define the population or universe to include all full-time or part-time students, discover where in the administration building there is a file containing one and only one I.B.M. card for each student, instruct an assistant to select a pure random sample of these cards, and then have the students so chosen interviewed anonymously about billiards on campus.

Probability samples may be random, stratified, cluster, multi-stage, or mixtures thereof. While all of these procedures are far superior methodologically to judgment samples, they are sometimes rather costly. And all suffer from the difficulty of obtaining complete and accurate lists of persons from which to draw members of the sample.

Simple Random Samples

Pure random sampling demands selection by chance alone. Each individual in the universe has an equal opportunity to enter the sample. Randomization is not accomplished, however, by being unsystematic or unorganized. The layman's so-called random sample, obtained by casually picking an accessible set of people, is in scientific terms a judgment sample; that is, he may not set out deliberately to select a group of people conforming to some characteristic (and therefore unrepresentative of the total population), but bias is an almost certain end product of his lack of system. Untrained persons, for example, hardly ever select for their sample representative proportions of the aged, the stay-at-homes, the gad-abouts, the immigrants, the rich, and the beatniks. As opposed to such unplanned, hit-or-miss methods, social scientists make careful efforts to insure that the determinative operator is chance, not convenience or pleasantness or enthusiasm.

Randomization is achieved by lot (the traditional slips of paper in a hat, which incidentally are surprisingly difficult to mix in an equalitarian fashion), by mechanical contrivances (well-balanced roulette wheels, playing cards), or by tables of random numbers. These tables, notably those developed and published by the Department of Statistics of the University of London in 1927[12] and 1939[13] and the Rand Corporation in 1955,[14] are lists of thoroughly scrambled numbers from which research workers read off, in any direction, randomly arranged digits.

Simple random samples have several desirable qualities. No advance knowledge of population characteristics is required. Accuracy is measurable because variability of a random sample follows the laws of probability. And random samples become increasingly representative of the entire population as they are enlarged—a property not shared by judgment samples. Disadvantages of chance-based samples are the need to identify every person, the likelihood of obtaining sample members who are widely dispersed geographically (thus requiring heavy transportation costs for interviewers), and the ever-present possibility of obtaining a nonrepresentative sample (a crippling defect were it not for the feasibility of measuring sampling variability). Yet the advantages so outweigh the defects that randomization has come to be considered essential to selecting a scientific, representative sample upon which to base reliable inferences about human and other populations. Randomization always occurs at the last step of any kind of probability sampling.

A popular substitute for pure random sampling is selection at regular intervals (say, every fourteenth name from a city directory or every ninth dwelling unit along a street), which goes by the name of systematic sampling. A systematic sample is sometimes random, sometimes stratified, and sometimes not a probability sample at all. In the unlikely event that the list or other array from which sample members are selected is randomly ordered, systematic sampling provides an efficient means of obtaining a random sample. Ordinarily the list is alphabetically, chronologically, geographically, or otherwise nonrandomly ordered, which at best eventuates in a sample stratified by ethnic derivation (reflected in initial letter of last names), order of arrival, location, and the like. At worst a judgment sample results, with the debilitating bias usual to the type; for instance, the above-mentioned street may have nine dwelling units in each block, thus introducing a systematic bias (the sample might contain only corner houses). For these reasons, systematic samples can be used only with especial discretion.

Stratified Samples

Stratified sampling consists of the selection of a group of random samples, one from each class or stratum of the population or universe. We first divide the universe into two or more strata or classes and then proceed to take a pure random sample within each stratum. The rationale underlying the division into classes is that we thereby guarantee that each stratum is reasonably well represented in the combined sample; for instance, if we stratify an undergraduate college by classes and then choose randomly 100 freshmen, 100 sophomores, 100 juniors, and 100 seniors, we have thus deliberately arranged our total sample of 400 so that no class is represented by fewer than 100 students. Considerable deviation from this balanced outcome is unlikely in a pure random sample of 400, but it is possible and occasionally does happen.

The example just given illustrates one type of stratified sample: equal allocation into strata. Two other common stratification procedures are employed: proportional and optimum allocation. Proportional stratification is characterized by selection of the same fraction from each stratum; that is, sample members are drawn from each stratum in the same proportion as members of that stratum occur in the universe. For example, a 5 per cent sample of the voters of a city may be selected by drawing a 5 per cent random sample from each of the city's wards, thus yielding a random sample stratified proportionally by wards.

A more sophisticated principle of stratified sampling is that of equalizing not numbers or proportions but sampling variability within each stratum. In this third type of stratification, the allocation of sample members chosen from each class of the population is determined by computing the variability (through estimating the mean and standard deviation or other statistical measures described in Chapter V) and then assigning to each stratum the number of cases calculated to be necessary to attain statistical significance (or a given confidence interval). For instance, interviewing people concerning their voting intentions might yield a 58 per cent preference for a candidate in urban areas and a 52 per cent preference for him in rural areas; an obvious question is whether the 8 and 2 per cent margins of prospective victory are really meaningful. The method of optimum allocation maximizes the likelihood that such percentages will be statistically useful. However, since this procedure is much more demanding than the proportional or equal allocation methods, it is the least commonly used. Still, it is the most efficient of the three, tending to avoid both the wastefulness of taking a larger sample than necessary from any stratum and the ruinousness of taking so small a sample from any stratum as to invalidate the results.

Stratification accomplishes several things: certainty that no essential groups are omitted from the sample, assurance that all such groups are represented by the minimum numbers set by the investigator, geographic concentration (usually) which reduces expense, and greater precision than is attained through simple random sampling. On the other hand, there are disadvantages: the necessity of knowing in advance the stratum occupied by each member of the population, and the labor of additional computations not required in simple random sampling. The larger the number of variables used in stratification, the more these strengths and weaknesses are accentuated.

Multi-stage Cluster Samples

Further accentuation of these same virtues and defects is obtained by using more complex sample designs, one of which is the subsample—that is, the procedure of taking a sample of the first sample. Carried through additional steps, continued subsampling yields what are called multi-stage samples. When the elementary sampling units of stratification are groups rather than individuals, the process is called cluster sampling. Multi-stage cluster samples are highly efficient though very difficult to design. Moreover, since their design costs are high and their performance costs are low, they are rarely justified for an ordinary one-shot study. But they may be ideal for a series of studies —as in the Current Population Survey conducted monthly by the United States Bureau of the Census.[15]

Consider a fictional and simplified illustration of a multi-stage cluster sample of the United States population. The fifty states are first grouped into three clusters: North, South, and West. In stage I, a single state is then selected randomly from each of the three regional clusters or strata. In each of these three states, we define three more clusters: metropolitan, other urban, and rural areas. In stage II, we select at random one geopolitical unit (city, town, county) from each of these three clusters in each state, thus stratifying additionally by degree of urbanization. Next, within each of the nine chosen areas we set up four clusters (of wards in the city and farming districts in the country) on the basis of social class: upper, middle, working, and lower. Stage III consists of randomly drawing one ward or district from each of these 36 socio-economic clusters. The final clustering is by education: we group individuals into college, high school, and elementary school clusters within each of the 36 stage III areas—a total of 108 clusters. In the concluding stage, IV, we choose five individuals in random fashion from each of the 108 clusters (three education clusters in each of the 36 areas). The final result of this lengthy process is a sample of 540 people stratified according to geographic region, degree of urbanization, socio-economic standing of their locale, and amount of education—a four-stage cluster sample. In practice, more than one variable is often used to define a cluster, so that a four-stage sample may be based on as many as several dozen variables.

The most difficult part of the design stems from the demand common to all probability samples that we be able to ascertain the exact probability of being included in the sample for every person in the entire population from which the sample is drawn. Hence, statisticians designing such samples are compelled to weight the sampling units at every stage (necessitated by the fact of unequal numbers of people in the various units) and to keep track of these interacting weights. No wonder then that in sample design we so readily accept Sophie Tucker's plaint: "A good man (statistician) nowadays is hard to find."

IV

Analyzing Data

*

The intimacy of the relation between the design and analysis phases of a research study was pointed out at the beginning of Chapter III. We now turn to that interrelation as an intermediate topic between data collection (Chapter III) and statistical techniques (Chapter V). Since good research design is prerequisite to good data analysis, it is appropriate to commence with some remarks concerning design.

Experimental and Control Groups

Scientific social research is an attempt to prove or disprove an hypothesis postulating a relation between two or more variables by controlling all relevant factors except the ones specified in the hypothesis. Thus the design is aimed at handling extraneous factors—to eliminate them, to minimize their effects, to have them cancel themselves out, or to facilitate removing them during data analysis.

The classic procedure is to expose some people to a stimulus (the experimental group) and to withhold it from others (the control group). If the two groups are approximately identical before exposure, except for the stimulus, differences between the groups after exposure may be attributed to the stimulus. This procedure can be varied by using several experimental groups, each exposed to a different stimulus, or by introducing several stimuli successively to the experimental group or groups. In Harold Gosnell's experiment on voting registration, nonpartisan notices stating the basic facts regarding registration (eligibility, time, place) were sent to the experimental group, followed by a second notice of exhortatory character; the control group received nothing. Later, the percentages registered in the experimental and control groups were compared. Since the two groups were roughly similar in national descent, proportion of males, economic circumstances, and political status, these factors could be ruled out as influences on experimental group-control group differences in registration.[1] However, this study shared with others an inability to equate all possible interfering variables in control and experimental groups; hence it was impossible to state with finality that only the leaflets were responsible for the observed larger proportion registered in the exposed group. Most studies concentrate on a few experimental variables (in this example, the leaflets) and a few controlled variables (here, nationality, sex, income, politics). But to cover the scores of potentially relevant variables, at least several and perhaps dozens of inquiries are necessary.

Experiments may be artificial or natural—arranged by the investigator himself or arranged for him by external conditions. Sociologists occasionally espouse pure, artificial experimentation: showing one company of soldiers a film on why they fight and sending another company out for the usual afternoon of close-order drill.[2] More common in sociology, however, is the self-generated study in which the stimulus for change is not introduced by the experimenter: say, examining the effects of social isolation not by isolating a child over a period of years but by studying one who is discovered to have been isolated.[3]

In addition to degree of artificiality, another contrast of approaches that may be available to social experimenters is between simultaneous and successional designs—that is, contemporaneous comparison of stimulus effects in two or more groups or chronological comparison of effects over time. A complete experiment provides for both simultaneous and longitudinal examination of effects.

Longitudinal Study Designs

Longitudinal studies are of two kinds: projected and *ex post facto*. Research folkways inherited from the physical sciences call for a projected design, in which the study begins immediately before introduction of the stimulus and concludes shortly after the effect is observed. In the previously cited military example, the social statistician appears at the camp, studies the personnel records of Companies A and B, interviews the men if necessary, shows the film to Company A and sends Company B to the drill field, re-examines both companies, and then leaves the area to work at his calculating machine. This beguiling scenario, however, is not always practical for studying long-range effects, which are likely to be both more attractive and more consequential for human endeavors. If we want to know the extent to which the effects of the film persevere after the soldiers are shipped overseas and engage the enemy, we may have to wait a year after showing the film—by which time it will be difficult, expensive, and tedious to locate and reinterview the now widely dispersed men; many will have transferred to other units, some will be in hospitals or cemeteries or prison camps, and some will be discharged. Furthermore, the delay of a year before results are known

—and therefore a year before they can be used—is undesirable.

The *ex post facto* design offers a way of handling these and other obstacles attendant upon lengthy intervals between exposure to the stimulus and measurement of the effect. This technique is distinguished by its superficially reversed time sequence: we begin at the end and end at the beginning. For example, to ascertain the effect of playing on a college athletic team on one's income twenty years after graduation, we would first interview in 1965 some college graduates of the class of 1945 concerning their incomes and then determine whether or not they participated in college athletics twenty years before. Note that the traditional research sequence is reversed; we start with the resultant phenomenon (income) and then trace it back to the antecedent condition (athletics). This reversal need not distort results but merely alters the chronology of data acquisition; thus if former footballer Archie Starcher earns half again as much money as the nonathlete Isidore Segogenblock, this fact is not changed by the order in which the information is secured. Used carefully and with discretion, the *ex post facto* design supplies valid and reliable data over a time span which poses a prohibitive barrier to the classic projected design. Provided that appropriate data have been collected and preserved from the pre-stimulus period, there is no limit to the chronological coverage of *ex post facto* studies. However, when pre-stimulus data are not available, thereby forcing reliance upon recollective questions, the *ex post facto* technique is not recommended.

Complete and Incomplete Designs

The moral of the preceding pages is that the ideal social research project conforms to the following model:

	BEFORE STIMULUS	AFTER STIMULUS	DIFFERENCE
Experimental group	x_1	x_2	$x_2 - x_1$
Control group	y_1	y_2	$y_2 - y_1$

The test of the stimulus resides in a comparison of the before-after difference in the experimental group with the before-after difference in the control group.[1] Frequently patience or resources do not permit designing and carrying to completion studies containing all four cells of the paradigm. Even so, such incomplete designs need not be disregarded as inherently unworthy of modern sociology.

The panel study, a simple successional experiment possessing only cells x_1 and x_2, is often useful. We may, for example, ask the same sample of voters every month about their voting preference—a sometimes excellent technique for recording opinion change because it identifies specifically which individuals change and which do not, in contrast to simply presenting totals as do other studies. However, repeated reinterviewing of the same persons may sensitize them unduly to the subject of the research, a defect called reinterviewing bias. There is still another disadvantage to the panel study: consider, for example, that we interview students at the first meeting of a sociology class concerning their attitudes toward dating and then reinterview the same students on the same subject at the end of the semester; lacking a control group, we can never be certain whether it was the sociology course or something else that induced whatever observed attitudinal differences might arise. Nonetheless, the simple successional design is used in both the social and physical sciences. In fact most physical science experiments omit the control group entirely on the presumption that the experimenter already knows what would happen if the stimulus were not applied.

Another incomplete design contains only cells x_2 and y_2. This simultaneous design may be exemplified by comparing attitudes held by fraternity men and independents concerning drinking to intoxication. Here is the traditional simple correlation analysis of one variable (fraternity status) against another (drinking). The stimulus consists of joining a fraternity. Again, however, we would have trouble imputing causation. Without matching x_1 against y_1, we could only state observed differences between x_2 and y_2; we could not attribute differences in attitude toward drinking to fraternity membership because of the prospect that uncontrolled variables are determinants.

Two other deviations from the classic design involve only one cell (x_2) or one cell plus quasi-accurate retrospective questions or plausible conjecture. The first case is simply a descriptive study of conditions at a given moment, useless for causal inference. The other design is no better; thus by imaginatively filling in cell x_1 with hypothetical recollections of their own yesterdays, men through the centuries have been able to "prove" that children no longer respect their parents as children once did and that the world is going to the dogs.

Finally there is the inadequate but common trend study comprised of repeated cross-sectional surveys, yielding a two-cell design, y_1 and x_2, from which no valid inferences may be drawn. Suppose we know that in 1965 the percentage of men in one group who prefer shaving with electric razors is exactly double the percentage in a different group who preferred electric razors in 1960. The incompleteness of design prevents knowing why the two groups differ. Perhaps electric razors are becoming more popular. Perhaps the second group preferred electric razors to the same extent in 1960 as in 1965. Perhaps the men in one group have heavier beards than those in the other. Again the findings are of descriptive value only—though it must be admitted that descriptive information is frequently of considerable utility.

Matching

An essential accompaniment to proper use of the before-after or longitudinal comparison in conjunction with the experimental-control or cross-sectional contrast is matching. Matching establishes the similarity of the experimental and control groups with regard to those variables deemed by the experimenter to have greatest potential relevance to the hypotheses. There are four ways to approach matching.

Precision matching consists of setting up pairings such that every person in the experimental group has an exact counterpart in the control group. Thus if the experimental group contains an unmarried Catholic male college graduate between 30 and 39 years of age working as a salesman, the control group must contain a member exactly equivalent in such factors. The difficulty of obtaining such precise matchings when as many as six variables are involved can be readily imagined, but the analytical advantages are sometimes worth the effort. When the relevant variables are clearly ascertainable and few in number, precision matching is highly effective. But since no attention is paid to any other variables, the selection of factors on which to base the matching is crucial: if the matched variables are poorly chosen, the matching may be worthless. Furthermore, dropouts are doubled in such a set-up: for each person lost to either group (through death, moving away, refusal to be interviewed, or other reasons), his counterpart in the other group also must be withdrawn.

Frequency matching consists of ensuring that the two groups are alike in total distribution of the relevant variables, but no attempt is made to locate exact individual pairs. This rendering equivalent of the numbers in each significant category is much easier, quicker, and cheaper than precision matching. And since it suffices to "hold other factors constant" between experimental and control groups, it is more often used than the more rigorous but easily disrupted precision control, despite its lack of the other method's virtue of reflecting combinations of variables.

A third approach is to match probabilistically through randomization. If both the experimental and control groups are pure random samples drawn from the same universe, and if the numbers are reasonably large, equalization of frequencies within classes is possible though, as the renowned English statistician R. A. Fisher has said, "always incomplete." Since the sociological researcher can never be certain that he has identified all possible confounding variables, insistence on precision or frequency matching to insure that samples are identical regarding every variable except that to be tested may be regarded as "a totally impossible requirement."[5] When potentially relevant variables are innumerable or elusive, randomization is the best procedure; when relevant interfering factors may be identified confidently, precision or frequency matching is preferable. Matching by randomization ordinarily requires larger samples than the other techniques, but the selection process is far simpler and faster.

After-the-fact matching is possible through analysis of covariance, a statistical technique which compensates final scores to allow for initial variations. It is used to cancel out a limited number of interfering variables by subtracting their effects after the experiment is performed. But although this questionable-sounding procedure is methodologically legitimate, its complicated aspect and ersatz quality render it useful only as an afterthought. Like the Broadway "play doctor," its primary utility lies in correcting earlier mistakes.

Measuring Stimulus Effects

Another methodological concern associated with experimental design is measurement of the effect of the stimulus. A pre-stimulus measurement is desirable to learn the extent to which the effect is present in each of the two groups before exposure; if the two groups are unevenly matched, allowance must be made in analysis and interpretation. After exposure to the stimulus, the effect must be remeasured. The presumed influence of the stimulus is the difference between the post- and pre-measures, with allowance for experimental-control group differences, if any.

After matching, exposure, and observation of effect, the investigator attempts to impute causal relations by specifying which of the persons responded in the crucial way, the part or parts of the stimulus complex to which they responded, the sequence of behavior leading to the effect, and the environmental conditions having a bearing on the results. Thus sociologists identify four modes of specification: population, stimulus, process, and situation. An example of each may aid comprehension. In the voting study cited above, Gosnell devoted most of his attention to differential responses according to socio-economic status, education, place of residence, voting experience, ethnic origin, and knowledge of government workings. The director of a new film for soldiers telling "Why We Fight" may profit from knowing which sound effects, visual themes, and verbal phrasings have been most effective in conveying pro-American or anti-enemy sentiments in previous films in the series. Specification of process is illustrated by an experiment in which students were asked to rank occupations, given fictitious rankings beforehand; probing uncovered that students who were told that other persons ranked politics high tended to think of statesmen while ranking the occupation "politician," whereas those told that politics ranked low selected ward heelers in making their own ranking.[6] In specifying the situation, the researcher asks what are the consequences of doing a voters' registration study in an election year or of soldiers' seeing a film under compulsion.

Qualified Accuracy

The classic experimental design with matched groups
and time sequence adds tremendously to scientists'
ability to draw conclusions, but it does not curb inaccuracy. Expectation of error is a hallmark of science.
And with this acknowledgment of inaccuracy comes a
strenuous effort toward greater precision.

One of the distinguishing characteristics of the scientific method is its built-in provision for error.[7] Scientists are taught early in their training that they cannot
make any statement wih absolute certainty and that
they should indicate the degree of confidence they
have in each statement. Thus, instead of saying that a
poll shows candidate A leading in pre-election results
with 53 per cent of the voters, we report that candidate
A gained 53 per cent $\pm$ 5 per cent of the respondents.
This 5 per cent error factor (measured as two times
the standard deviation—see Chapter V) is a way of
informing the reader approximately how much the results need to be qualified. Since the indicated range,
48 to 58 per cent, overlaps the crucial 50 per cent level,
we infer that the election is far from settled—a conclusion not implicit in the bald 53 per cent statement.

Bias and Sampling Errors

There are many ways in which error may creep into
interview and questionnaire surveys. Most of them do
so under the heading of bias. Errors of bias are those
arising through carelessness, incompetence, or poor
judgment. And although not inevitable, they are always possible. Bias is found in complete enumerations
as well as in samples. This kind of error is corrected
by being more thorough, hiring better interviewers and
supervisors, planning the study design more rigorously,
being more careful in recording and tabulating responses, improving analytical operations, and so forth.

Such errors are systematic and hence not self-cancelling.

Another type of error is introduced whenever one samples. Variability is inherent in the sampling process and cannot be eliminated without taking a complete enumeration. However, if one takes a probability sample, the magnitude and direction of the sampling error can be calculated. With increased sample size, the sampling error diminishes steadily and predictably. In sum, their greater obviousness and our ability to compute their amount make sampling errors far more tractable than bias, which is often deceptively difficult to detect and can rarely be measured and hence allowed for.

Although size of sample is relevant to sampling error, such is not the case with bias. Biases can never be corrected simply by enlarging the sample, as doubling the sample merely adds another dose of what is probably the same degree of error. For this reason, sheer hugeness of a sample does not guarantee correct results. Consider the classic illustration of the *Literary Digest* Presidential election poll of 1936, which underestimated the popular vote of the winner by 20 per cent despite the impressive sample size of 2,400,000 ballots. In contrast to this debacle, a *Fortune* magazine poll of the same year, based on only 4,500 cases, came within 1 per cent of predicting the actual vote. In fact, it is much better to have a representative small sample than a nonrepresentative large one. "The millions of cases in the *Digest* poll were less predictive than a sample of fewer than 100 cases would have been if chosen by proper sampling procedure from a representative group of the electorate."[8]

Personal Influence and Sociometry

Prospects of bias and sampling variability are implicit in all research techniques for gathering data, analyzing data, or both—as in sociometry, content analysis, and related methods of assessing interpersonal influence, attitudes, and communication. The size of the group under study is sufficiently important to demand a variety of research skills: in small groups, sociometry can be used to identify cliques, social cleavages, isolates, social climbers, and leaders; in studying large groups, sociologists turn to latent structure analysis and several tools for examining mass communications, such as content analysis. In any case, simple inspection of the formal organization of a group is insufficient to an understanding of how decisions are achieved, actions are taken, leaders are followed, hatreds are solidified, and information is disseminated.

Sociometry charts interpersonal relations, showing in one or more diagrams the friendship and avoidance patterns in a group. Sociograms present graphically these attractions and rejections of each person toward each other person in the group through use of solid and dotted lines connecting circles and squares representing persons. When the group is large and the interrelationships numerous, a tabular form of presentation called a sociometric matrix may be used. Since its invention by J. L. Moreno in 1934,[9] the sociogram has been applied by many scholars in such diversified contexts as school classes, prison groups, work crews in factories and offices, military squads, and teenage cliques. Though cumbersomeness generally confines its use to groups numbering fewer than fifty people, sociometry has been applied to the analysis of two or three hundred people at once.[10] The grist for sociometric charting is supplied either by direct observation or through interviewing. This research tool is particularly useful in studying leadership, friendship formation, and discrimination in small groups. Regrettably, however, its dramatic appeal, its seeming readiness of use, and its appearance of objectivity have encouraged its adoption by sociological amateurs, with a consequently greater frequency of misuse than is the case with most sociological research devices.

Attitude Analysis

When the group membership exceeds several hundred persons, different approaches must be applied to the study of group behavior and individual attitudes. Appreciation of the place of personal relationships in determining which members of a local community play influential roles in attitude formation and social action requires examination of values and attitudes, social stratification, status, folkways and mores, manifest and latent functions of the various subgroups within the community, and other topics mentioned in Chapter I. Certain special research procedures may be introduced, such as latent structure analysis, produced by Paul F. Lazarsfeld during and since World War II, and factor analysis, an older technique dating from the 1920's, both of which indirectly measure fundamental but unobservable variables from less profound but observable variables.[11] Both latent structure analysis and factor analysis have uses ranging far beyond the present context and even beyond the normal boundaries of sociology and psychology. These laborious mathematical models reduce a number of relatively superficial though directly visible factors to a few underlying factors (or sometimes a single factor) that can represent more or less completely the entire observed set. Factor analysis proceeds from a matrix of intercorrelations between each variable and every other one, while latent structure analysis is based on a probability matrix—circumstances indicative of their toilsome but intellectually sophisticated nature.

Latent structure analysis is cousin to the scaling techniques mentioned in the final section of this chapter. Like other scaling procedures, it is frequently used to examine interpersonal communication, including both the formation and maintenance of attitudes and the expression of facts and ideas through formal media of communication—the latter focus being shared with content analysis.

Content Analysis

Content analysis—as its name implies—identifies, describes, and analyzes in detail the components of verbal or pictorial material in an objective, systematic, and quantitative manner. It asks much the same questions as the reporter writing the lead paragraph of a newspaper story: who, what, when, where, why, and so what? Everyone who thoughtfully reads or listens to any communication performs something of the same process; the special contribution of content analysis is its addition of quantification to perception, precision to insight. It shares with many other sociological research tools the quality of doing more objectively, precisely, and thoroughly what intelligent and educated laymen do anyway. For instance, anyone in 1948 who carefully read a variety of newspaper accounts of the denunciation, security hearings, and final clearance of Federal official Edward U. Condon would have perceived differential treatment of the case in different papers. But by examining all news articles mentioning Condon in all issues of the nine major New York newspapers from March 1948 through October 1948, classifying or specifying every statement in each article as to degree of favorableness to Condon, source of information, repetitiveness, vagueness, and so on, two sociologists were able to show the manner and extent to which the various papers exhibited highly different coverage of and attitudes toward the case, despite the fact that all were ostensibly reporting the same story. Taking the broadest finding as an example, the proportion of pro-Condon statements varied from 65 per cent in the *Times* to 18 per cent in the *Journal-American,* with the other seven papers ranged in between.[12]

Content analysis can be applied to a great variety of problems, including such questions as who actually wrote the plays attributed to Shakespeare and certain publications credited to Mark Twain.[13] By breaking down the content of the communication (in these cases published, but in others personal diaries or recorded dialogue) into the smallest meaningful units of information, social statisticians measure themes and tendencies in the message. Examples of content analysis concerning authorship are frequencies of appearance of various words, lengths of sentences, and other elements comprising literary style.

Sociologists also analyze such media as magazine fiction and comic strips to ascertain values and attitudes. In 1946, Bernard Berelson and Patricia Salter examined 198 short stories in eight popular magazines regarding ethnic designation of heroes, villains, and other characters as associated with social class, stereotyping, aspirations, and so forth. In those short stories, WASPs (white Anglo-Saxon Protestants) consistently received better treatment on virtually every index than did minority groups and foreigners. "Negroes and Jews never appeared as heroes or heroines. No Negroes or Jews were depicted as members of the armed forces. They had the lowest occupational rating. They constituted the only group with more disapproved than approved traits."[14]

From the kinds of friends and enemies chosen for Little Orphan Annie and the denouements provided them from 1948 through 1950, Lyle Shannon concluded that Annie "approves the symbols which have traditionally represented good in our society" and "condemns some of the well known sins," reflecting generally "the conservative social idealism of the middle class" and reliance on "faith, hope, and charity—but not too much charity." Annie and her friends are for "the church, truth, hard work, and pressure when necessary in order to get what one wants" and opposed to "crooks, politicians, slowness in government, and foreigners who would like U.S. military secrets."[15] No wonder this comic strip is so often picked to illustrate calcified Americanism and copy-book virtues.

Both Shannon and Berelson-Salter measured authors' intentions by classifying and counting the writers' selection and treatment of characters, situations, and resolution of conflicts. When such a classification is systematized, it becomes a scale.

Scales and Indexes

Sociologists often wish to order a series of items in a meaningful sequence or scale. Studies of attitudes and other phenomena frequently make use of scales: IQ, mechanical aptitude, social distance, dominance-submission, socioeconomic status, political interest, cost of living, and many others. Consequently a number of scaling methods have been developed, of which three are discussed here.

L. L. Thurstone has evolved the most widely used method of scaling attitudes. In his method of equal-appearing intervals, many statements are gathered from widely scattered sources, placed on slips of paper, and then shown to several dozen judges, who are instructed to place them in, say, seven or eleven piles representing a graduated series of attitudes. These sortings into piles are then tabulated and evaluated statistically. The final scale consists of the least ambiguous items (those with the smallest variations), arranged into a graded series from one extreme through moderate to the other extreme.[16] Rensis Likert advocated a technique similar to Thurstone's, but one differing in the manner of determining scale values.[17] Both procedures, however, seek to identify those statements which discriminate most clearly between respondents falling at each end of the scale. Thus, in a test of attitudes toward the United Nations, the items chosen should elicit highly different responses from subjects having opposed attitudes toward the U.N.; statements which do not discriminate clearly between pro- and anti-United Nations respondents are discarded.

The scalogram method originated by Louis Guttman attempts more than the Thurstone and Likert techniques, but it is not always applicable. The most ambitious attribute of scale analysis is the notion of reproducibility. If an attitude is "scalable," then knowledge of a person's over-all score enables the investigator to infer correctly how that individual responded to each of the component items in the scale. For instance, if a set of six attitude questions concerning the United Nations is scalable, we could reproduce from each person's final score just how he answered each of the six questions. As might be surmised, perfect reproducibility is rarely attained. A coefficient of reproducibility of .90 is considered acceptable; smaller coefficients cause the scale to be abandoned.[18]

Scales are classifiable into four levels; in ascending order of precision, they are nominal, ordinal, interval, and absolute.[19] Nominal scales are simple typologies of two or more categories without rank, as men and women. Ordinal scales contain the added property of ranking, as in Thurber's scale of "people to whom other people send Christmas cards": relatives, intimate friends, friends, acquaintances, mere acquaintances, and persons one has only met once.[20] Interval scales have precise units of measurement, so that we can specify distances between points on the scale; for example, a Fahrenheit temperature of 90 is as far above one of 70 as the latter exceeds 50 degrees. An absolute or ratio scale contains all of the above properties plus the additional one of a zero point, which permits us to say that A is twice as large as B or Jane is twice as tall as Gwendolyn. To illustrate with a single variable, age may be classified into the following scales: nominal—people of determinable age, people of unknown age; ordinal—children, young adults, mature adults, aged; interval—one year older than I am, two years older, three years older, and so on; and absolute—0-9 years old, 10-19 years old, 20-29 years old, and so forth.

An index number is "a one-dimensional measurement of a more-dimensional object. This is achieved by either having one of the dimensions represent the total, or by an index formula that combines two or more dimensions into one figure."[21] The combined index number represents several component variables related to the complex quality being measured. Let us consider three examples, one in which both approaches are used, one in which a combined index is customary, and one in which the single variable is usual. A food cost index may be prepared by using the price of a single food (beef, bread) or by computing a weighted composite of beef, pork, bread, sugar, oranges, chocolate, coffee, corn, asparagus, and the like. The latter index is obviously more sophisticated, though more difficult. Second, an index of beauty rarely is based on a single trait; rather, beauty contest judges base decisions on the combined impact of face, torso, hips, posture, legs, and personality. Some contests even supply judges with an index formula in which contestants are scored o through 10 for each trait, the winner being the girl achieving the greatest total score. Third, baseball batting proficiency is most often measured by a single variable, though fans cannot agree on which one to use: batting average, home runs, runs batted in, or some other indicator. In his younger days, the author of this book invented a composite index, the bases advanced percentage, but declined to publicize it on the assumption that it was too complicated to be understood by most fans and too difficult for sports writers and announcers to use—although hardly too tedious for baseball statisticians to compute. Not all statisticians admire index numbers anyway. As M. J. Moroney fumed: "When I think of these curses on modern civilization I feel in me the spirit of St. George and I long to dash into battle with this dragon of superstition which ensnares so many young maidens in the pit of idle computation."[22]

Masculine protectiveness toward frail femininity notwithstanding, statistical computations do serve a noble and lordly quest: the acquisition, elaboration, and substantiation of genuine social facts. The next chapter deals with the statistical operations employed by journeyman sociologists, followed by a discussion of electronic computers and mathematical models in sociology.

Statistical Operations

＊

The mathematical skills of adding and multiplying and the mechanical assistance of the desk calculator and the I.B.M. computer are supplemented in social science research by a set of operations, sometimes quantitative and sometimes not, that have come to be designated as statistics. Statistics are used to construct tables, prepare charts, compute averages and correlations, fit curves, make estimates from samples, and test hypotheses.

Statistics is a valuable instrument that belongs in the little black bag of every nonmedical doctor and educated man. Indeed, we are rapidly approaching the time when the general public will find knowledge of elementary statistics as essential as the ability to make change. Despite the popular image and auto-paralysis that teaches us to fear, loathe, and remain illiterate about numbers, statistics is an innocuous subject, as indispensable as grammar and possibly easier to learn.

Sociologists who wish to merit the label "scientist" have no choice in the matter. As a condition of obtaining the Ph.D., they learn the rudiments of statistics and often its intricacies. Professional sociologists need to be literate in statistics at least as much as they need to be able to read a foreign language. Otherwise the lucid quantities and clever statistical artifacts of the trade are unintelligible. Thus the modern sociologist, whether he likes it or not—and many do not—learns the difference between the mean and the median in much the same spirit as the lawyer studies legal precedents and the garage mechanic buys a torque wrench.

Description and Inference

Statistics has two functions: to describe a set of data and to direct inferences from those data. Descriptive statistics is an attempt to make explicit the story implicit in collected data. To this end, statisticians condense masses of data into tables and diagrams which, properly presented, help identify trends and relationships. Tables and graphs have the advantage over prose descriptions in being able to convey considerably more information in a given space. Further concentration is achieved by the computing of percentages, ratios, indexes, rates, averages, and deviations which summarize the unwieldy, confusing, and generally incomprehensible raw data. Such measures supply information more quickly and less ambiguously than simply listing observed facts. A cost of living index summarizes in a single figure perhaps fifty commodity prices. The relative amounts of schooling of residents of New York and Louisiana may be compared most simply and speedily (though, as is seen later, not so completely) by use of an average, which summarizes in one figure the educational levels of the millions of residents of each state. Examining raw data even for smaller areas would be extremely tedious; imagine reading a series of numbers stating the years of schooling for each adult in a city of 25,000: 14, 9, 13, 5, 7, 17,

6, 10, 12, 15, 12, 8, 2, 9, 10, and so on, well past the onset of boredom and inattention.

Inductive statistics has a different purpose. Though financial and other limitations often compel sociologists to study a sample of 700 people rather than an entire city of 700,000, they are not content with knowing only descriptive facts about the 700. Ordinarily the reason for doing the research in the first place is to learn something about all the inhabitants of the city, not just about 700 of them. Therefore the researchers want to be able to generalize from the sample to the whole populace. Such generalization or inductive reasoning is possible through computation of the standard error, confidence intervals, and significance levels discussed in the last half of this chapter. If, and only if, a probability sample is taken, these measures may be computed. Then the signal superiority of probability over judgment sampling becomes evident.

Inferential statistics thus goes a giant step beyond the simpler accomplishments of descriptive statistics. But the inferential magic is bought at a price: it lacks the certainty of a simple descriptive fact. Also, as might be surmised, inductive statistics makes greater mathematical demands on the user. Since descriptive measures are easier to master and prerequisite to understanding the newer and more powerful inductive measures, they will now be considered first.

Figures and Graphs

Surely all readers are familiar with the sight if not the nomenclature of the more common modes of graphic presentation: the pie chart with its dessert-shaped wedges explaining where our tax dollar goes, the pictogram with sketches of airplanes or money bags, the line graph showing upward and downward stock market trends since 1929, the bar chart with its pillars depicting regional differences in soft drink consumption, the map with dots or shading in various colors to portray degrees of racial integration of public facilities, the flow chart identifying commuting paths, and the centrograph picturing focal points of population in 1960 versus 1790. In addition to the innumerable subtle variations of these diagrams, four other graphs are of particular interest for social research.

The histogram, a series of parallel vertical bars, received its statistical baptism from Karl Pearson in 1895. The frequency polygon is a jagged curve formed by connecting a set of plotted points. When a frequency polygon is made more regular, the rounded line is called a smooth or smoothed curve. Finally, data are sometimes plotted on graph paper having a logarithmic or graduated scale, an especially useful format when analyzing rates of change.

Scholars writing up their research have a choice between charts and tables. They tend to choose the former when their intent is primarily to portray data in a way that the reader will find attractive or stimulating. The single-mindedness of most graphs also carries with it an intellectual or emotional impact far exceeding that of a table. Tables are used when the writer is striving for detail or accuracy. The visual appeal of a chart catches the reader's eye and identifies major trends with maximum conviction, but few graphs supply the exactitude, extensiveness, or fragmentation of a good table. On the other hand, tables may present several decimal places and many rows and columns (equivalent fractionization would clutter up a graph to the point of unreadability), and they are unsurpassed at unemotionally conveying research findings.

Univariate and Bivariate Tables

In statistical tables, raw data are grouped into qualitative categories or quantitative class intervals by determining the number of cases falling into each group. As with graphs, this second form of presentation and analysis also may be approached naïvely with some success or sophisticatedly with greater reward.

A univariate table tells the frequency in each of several classes, as for instance a certain town contains 98 no-car families, 76 one-car families, 54 two-car families, 32 three-car families, and 10 four-or-more-car families. A bivariate table presents joint frequencies of occurrence, with one variable arranged horizontally and the other vertically. In comparing milk and beer consumption in the hypothetical example that follows, the number in each cell or compartment indicates how many people are in the milk and beer drinking combination designated by row and column headings. For example, the upper left cell has an entry of 13, signifying that 13 people drink zero quarts of either milk or beer daily.

Quarts of beer consumed per day

		0	1	2	3 or more	Total
Quarts	0	13	2	1	27	43
of milk	1	18	5	2	16	41
consumed	2	8	4	2	3	17
per day	3 or more	49	18	0	0	67
	Total	88	29	5	46	168

Clearly these 168 people drink more milk than beer, though no one is a heavy imbiber of both.

Multi-variate tables incorporate a third variable into columnar divisions within the classes of one of the other variables. Champagne drinking might be included as a third variable by installing four additional columns inside each of the beer consumption columns, representing 0, 1, and 2 or more-bottle champagne drinkers, and their total; thus there would be, including all totals, twenty columns and five rows in this trivariate table. If a desire for simplicity motivates omission of the totals (they can always be found by addition), the table would contain twelve columns and four rows—a four-by-four-by-three or forty-eight-fold table. If Scotch drinking (in, say, five classes) were included as a fourth variable, the table would then contain 240 cells, perhaps making it so complicated to read as to encourage "a wee droppie o' it."

Contingency tables showing the association between two qualitative attributes rarely exceed five classes in each direction and are often two-by-two or four-fold. Take as an example marital versus financial status (married or unmarried versus solvent or broke); inside the table there would be four cells representing, in turn, the numbers of persons who are married and solvent, unmarried and solvent, married and broke, or unmarried and broke.

Tables have case study as well as statistical uses. Consider this two-by-two table implying a strong relation between wealth and educational level.

	Educated	Uneducated	Total
Rich	12	1	13
Poor	1	12	13
Total	13	13	26

The uneducated rich man and the educated poor one are obviously exceptions to the over-all relation; intensive case studies might explain why these two people deviate from the statistical norm, presumably helping to clarify the wealth-education association.

Another hypothetical example of deviant case analysis concerns a study of education and mass media showing that educated people generally prefer printed as opposed to oral material, whereas uneducated persons turn to radio or television in preference to periodicals or books. However, the deviant cases or exceptions to this generalization would bother the researcher and might motivate introduction of a third variable: reading skill. Further examination then could disclose that those educated persons who prefer electronic media are poor readers, while the uneducated people who choose print are good readers. Defining the independent variable as reading ability instead of education means that the deviant cases are better understood and the whole situation clarified.

Averages

As was pointed out at the beginning of this chapter, social scientists often need to simplify data. No one looks forward to confronting a huge list of numbers to be waded through one-by-one and somehow comprehended en masse. Even as much as people like money, the prospect of merely reading a list of 50 million incomes of United States families is mildly terrifying. Hence the attractiveness of simplifying. Both the displeasure and the inefficiency of inspecting the entire batch of data are minimized by calculating a set of summarizing measures. The tendency to gather about a center is measured by an average (which is discussed in the next paragraph). But since the data are rarely concentrated at one spot, a measure of spread or dispersion is also needed. These two figures in turn may be supplemented by other descriptive numbers which have enough in common to be referred to as the moment system, a set of four indicators or parameters supplying a remarkably complete description of a distribution—even one containing 50 million incomes.

An average is a single central value used to represent a set of data. There are three widely used and five relatively rare kinds of averages. Social scientists wishing to describe data by means of an average have to know the properties of the various averages in order to be able to select the one most appropriate to each set of data. Incorrect choice of measure may result in distorted description.

The simplest measure of central tendency is the mode—that is, the value which occurs most frequently. The operative word here is typicality; for much the same reason, prevailing clothing styles are called modish.

The median is the value of the middle item in rank order. If five people line up in order of height, the median height is that of the third person. The median for six people lies halfway between the third and fourth. In sum, it is an average of position.

The best known average is the arithmetic mean; indeed, some people think that the mean is the only average. It is computed by adding together all of the values and dividing by the number of cases. For various mathematical and practical reasons, the mean is usually the most valuable measure of the three.

For comparison and illustration of these three terms, consider the amount of folding money carried by each of seven people: $2, $2, $5, $6, $10, $20, and $25. The mode is $2, the median $6, and the mean $10. Each average tells something different about the group: more of the people have $2 than any other sum; the man in the middle has $6; and if all seven pooled their greenbacks and redivided them equally, each would have $10.

Though the mode, median, or mean is usually sufficient to describe the central tendency of a set of data, sometimes another measure is preferable. For instance, none of the three major measures is adequate to explain why mileage driven always seems less than one's average speed implies it should be. The blame lies in use of an inapplicable average (the arithmetic mean) in place of the appropriate one (the less known and more toilsome harmonic mean). Popular allegations to the contrary, it is not that statistics lie, but rather that statistically ignorant—or in other cases, unscrupulous—persons use statistics improperly.

Variation

It should now be evident that no one measure of central tendency is adequate to all situations. Nor do all of the averages together suffice for a thorough description of a collection of observations. For this reason, statisticians qualify the average with a measure of dispersion or variation away from the center. For instance, Wichita and Milwaukee have an identical mean annual precipitation of 29.64 inches, but no farmer would be content to know simply the annual average. Monthly means for Milwaukee vary from 1.60 in December to 3.52 in September, and for Wichita from .64 in January to 4.69 in May.[1] Obviously variation between months is much greater in Wichita.

The difference between the monthly extremes is 4.05 inches in Wichita and 1.92 inches in Milwaukee. These measures of scatter or spread are called ranges. The range in height of students at Hullabaloo High is found by subtracting the height of the shortest, four feet seven inches, from that of the tallest, six feet eight inches—a variation of two feet one inch. But while the range is useful in many situations (deciding how much anti-freeze to put in your car or knowing the warmest and lightest clothing you need to pack for a trip), it is too simple for serious scholarly application, since it neglects all variation except that of the highest and lowest cases.

The pre-eminent measure of variation is the standard deviation—that is, the square root of the mean of the squares of the deviations about the mean. This regrettably unwieldy English phrasing illustrates a recurring theme: ideas that are easily understood when couched in mathematical language sound forbidding when expressed in English prose. But the inability of many persons to read mathematical symbols often forces us to state statistical notions in words—a format never intended to express mathematical thoughts, and one in which they do appear strange and unwieldy. Yet however expressed, the standard deviation is a cornerstone of sociological research. It is one of the most informative implements of descriptive statistics (for example, in using standard scores to compare apples with oranges or grades in chemistry with those in physical education) as well as of inferential statistics.

The Moment System

The foremost measure of central tendency—the mean —and the leading measure of dispersion—the standard deviation—form two parts of a coherent system to explore the structure of any frequency distribution. The mean corresponds to the first moment; the standard deviation indicates the second moment; and the third and fourth moments, known respectively as skewness and kurtosis, are measures of lopsidedness and flatness-peakedness. Just as the standard deviation supplements the mean, so the higher moments add further knowledge about a distribution. The entire set of moments ordinarily describes the distribution completely and exactly. The moments are also known as parameters.

Skewness, the third moment, measures distortion from symmetry. To say that a bell-shaped curve (or its tabular equivalent) is skewed to the right (or toward the higher values) means that the curve has a long tail extending toward the right edge of the graph. Take as an example the familiar distribution of personal incomes: most people are clustered in the lower income groups (ordinarily placed near the left margin of the graph), with diminishing numbers of persons represented among the higher income categories proceeding outward to the right side of the figure.

Kurtosis, the fourth moment, measures archedness. Normal curves are termed mesokurtic, or moderately arched. Flat-topped curves are called platykurtic, from the platypus, a squat creature with short tail. Peaked curves are termed leptokurtic, from the kangaroo which has a long tail and "leps."* Fifth and higher moments are computable but not readily interpreted.

---

* These curious explanations were contributed by W. S. Gossett, one of the greatest statisticians of all time, who wrote

Correlation and Regression

The four ingredients of the moment system identify the distinctive attributes of any distribution containing a single variable. However, sociologists frequently complicate matters by working with two or more variables at once. They may wonder, for example, whether there is any association between broken marriages and juvenile delinquency, between social class and which television programs one watches, or between choice of reference group and attitude toward baseball. Such situations call for correlation analysis: graphing a scatter diagram, plotting a regression line, and computing a correlation coefficient—all three of which elements are closely interrelated.

A scatter diagram is a set of dots portraying simultaneously the individual scores according to two variables, one measured along the horizontal axis and the other on the vertical axis. If a trend is discernible in the scatter diagram, it may be summarized geometrically by a regression line, which represents the scattered dots with a single straight or curving line coming as close to as many of the dots as possible; sometimes, however, the scattering is so irregular that drawing a regression line is not warranted. Correlation coefficients, which vary from .00 to 1.00, state the amount of association; direction is indicated by plus and minus signs symbolizing, respectively, direct and inverse relations. In a direct relationship, one variable tends to increase whenever the other increases (for example, the higher a person's educational level, the more professional his occupation tends to be); in an inverse relation, one variable increases as the other decreases (for example, the faster one drives his car above the

under the pseudonym of "Student" because of a company rule that employees could not publish articles under their own names. Since the company was the Guinness brewery in Dublin, it is possible that Gossett consumed too much of his own ale before publishing these ingenious and ingenuous explanations.

maximum torque r.p.m. in high gear, the lower the miles per gallon of gasoline).

Thorough correlation analysis requires use of all three of these indicators in order to take advantage of the virtues of each and yet not be confined to the vices of any one. The scatter diagram, like other graphic forms, offers immediate and forceful impact plus the less colorful but more utilitarian quality of saying exactly what it means. The regression line simplifies description and lends itself—though only with proper use —to prediction. The coefficient of correlation evaluates numerically the degree of association between two variables, but like most one-number representations of an entire distribution, it sometimes conceals significant fluctuations and eccentricities and thus lends itself to overemphasis and abuse by amateur statisticians eager to jump to a quantitative conclusion in order to get on with the fun of qualitative interpretation. Because the correlation coefficient makes exact statements, it may lull the quasi-knowledgeable user into a false sense of validity, unlike the apparently less sophisticated scatter diagram which humbly portrays the relation with little semblance of accuracy but with far more fidelity to facts. Finally, the most important fact to know about correlation analysis—whether involving scatter, regression, coefficient, or all three—is that it only measures co-variation and does not prove causation; identification of causes proceeds through experimental design and intimate knowledge of the subject at hand.

Analysis of the interrelation between two variables is called simple correlation. Introduction of one or more additional variables demands multiple correlation—measurement of the association between one dependent variable and two or more independent variables. When one or more of several independent variables is held constant, partial correlation is involved. Social scientists trying to ascertain why soldiers in World War II did or did not desert during combat examined three independent variables (feeling of fear, presence of an observer, and marital status) by multiple and partial correlation analysis. Multiple correlation, in its simplest form, compared tendency to desert under two conditions: all three independent variables favorable (afraid, no observer, married) versus all variables unfavorable (not afraid, observer present, single). Partial correlation was used to evaluate the tendency to desert as influenced by one independent variable when the other two variables were eliminated from consideration (the familiar "other factors being equal" situation).[2]

Curve Fitting

Closely allied to regression is the fitting of curves. If observed data are plotted in a scatter diagram, a trend may sometimes be detected—upward, downward, curving. For both presentational and analytical purposes, it is helpful to portray the trend by a single line. Use of a line inevitably simplifies description; the rationale is analogous to that of the average—with many of its strengths and weaknesses. The analogy may also be extended to variation, for statisticians have learned to evaluate the "goodness of fit," or the accuracy with which the line represents the scattered data. Curves are fitted by freehand or mechanically aided inspection or by mathematical formulas.

Curve fitting is not only complicated but easily misunderstood. Novices laboriously toiling through solutions to simultaneous equations and finally plotting the resultant curve are often inclined to believe they have achieved a less arbitrary fit than the person who simply sketches a curve unaided by formulas and calculators. To be sure, once the formal curve is chosen (straight line, logistic, parabola, and so forth), the result is objective. But someone must select the type of curve in the first place, and how can one be sure that a second degree parabola is superior to a logistic in the problem at hand? An algebraic equation or geometric curve (two ways of expressing the same thing) shows the relation between two variables only so far as it is possible to do so within the limitations of the particular equation used. Furthermore, the fact that a certain equation can reproduce a given relation is no proof that the equation really expresses the underlying nature of the relation.[3] In short, let the user beware.

Another temptation lies in extrapolation, the extension of a trend beyond the limits of observed data. All extrapolations have one insurmountable defect: there simply is no necessary connection between the closeness of fit of a curve to past observations and its accuracy in forecasting. A curve may fit precisely the data for the past one hundred years and yet fail to predict the situation for the next year.[4] Take the case of a leading statistician who tried to find "barometer" townships in Iowa which resembled the entire state in a number of characteristics. He identified certain areas, but examination of similar data for later years showed little correspondence between the barometer districts and the state as a whole. He was forced to conclude that the townships so chosen could be used only for the year for which the matchings were made.[5]

The Magic of Induction

Graphs, tables, averages, deviations, correlations, and curves form the foundation of descriptive statistics. Inferential statistics adopts these measures as a take-off platform in soaring to another level. Here a new world emerges, for whereas descriptive statistics merely does more precisely what nonstatisticians can do anyway, inductive statistics enables researchers to perform new tricks. The discovery of this fresh idea offering new power is perhaps best understood by analogy with Keats' "charmed magic casements, opening on the foam of perilous seas, in faery lands forlorn"; it is akin to sculpture and music describing unverbalizable worlds, dissection of matter and energy through physics, and the grasp of change and rate of change made possible by integral calculus.

This may appear to be heady company for the statistician, but his turns of magic can rival theirs. Indeed, any enhancement of man's ability to generalize from the particular to the universal is a contribution of inestimable value. Without induction we are stuck in the sands of literalness, limited to what we can encompass completely and forbidden to infer from the known sample to the semi-known universe.

Sampling inference is a form of inductive reasoning, an inherently inexact and hazardous process. One important function of statistics is to provide techniques for making inductive inferences and for measuring the degree of uncertainty in such inferences.[6] Uncertainty is computed through use of the theory of probability. If a sample is truly random, statisticians know how to compute the probability of error of the inference, but since the theory of probability is not applicable to non-random or judgment samples, investigators must take great care to ensure meeting the canons of probability sampling.

Probability and Set Theory

Although there is much truth in Laplace's observation that "the theory of probability is nothing more than good common sense adapted to calculation,"[7] the transition from the verbal logic of common sense to formal mathematics is barricaded with obstacles—so much so that a major task of instructors of social statistics is to overcome the emotional blocks that impede learning. In the last few years a new approach has begun to revolutionize the teaching of mathematics and statistics on all levels—from elementary school through graduate school. This new ascendant is called set theory. "It has been said that the whole of contemporary mathematics can be derived from the concept of a set and the rules of logic."[8]

A set is a collection of anything: objects, animals, thoughts, or symbols. We can speak of the set of all the inhabitants of Ishpeming, the set of all novels about the Civil War, the set of all straight lines passing through a given point, the set of all sheep people count when trying to go to sleep, and the set of all space ships in science-fiction magazines. Schematic sketching of the universe and its component sets and subsets, showing areas of overlap or intersection, aids comprehension and communication of the interrelationships among groups of persons.

Taking a sample consists of selecting a subset from a set. Thus a sample of 400 residents of Parsons, Kansas, interviewed concerning their attitudes toward Dixieland music, may be regarded as a subset containing 400 of Parsons' approximately 14,000 population. If interviewers obtain the sample members by collaring shoppers downtown, some of the 400 may not be Parsons residents. Thus the supposed subset will not be entirely contained in the set being studied, which partially invalidates the results. A properly designed and conducted random sample would ensure that all 400 sample members were elements of the target set of 14,000 Parsons residents—and also that all 14,000 elements of the target set would be equally likely to be included in the sample. When these conditions are met, a number of theorems and the algebra of sets (Boolean algebra) are brought into play to enhance the manipulability and generalizability of the subset data.[9]

Probability is defined in terms of the points or elements within sets and subsets. The probability of an event (symbolized graphically by a subset in a Venn diagram of interlocking circles) is the sum of the probabilities of all the sample points within that subset divided by the sum of all the sample points in the entire set.[10] For example, if a Las Vegas dealer wishes to draw a certain card from a deck, he is presented with fifty-two possible outcomes. Each outcome may be represented as a point, and the entire set might be viewed as being comprised of four subsets (spades, hearts, diamonds, and clubs), each containing thirteen sample points or elements. Diagrammatically, the fifty-two sample points may be placed in four columns, one for each suit, and thirteen rows, one for each card number (ace through ten) or face card (jack, queen, king). The probability of drawing any given type of card may be determined easily by counting the number of elements in the given subset and then dividing by fifty-two.

Estimation and Confidence

Given a probability sample, social scientists are able to derive estimates concerning the population from which the sample was drawn. Sometimes the estimate has a single value—as, for example, 12 of every 100 children in Springfield Elementary School cannot correctly identify Abraham Lincoln. More often a band or span is estimated—as, between 10 and 14 of every 100 children cannot identify Lincoln. Point or single-valued estimates are not fully meaningful because they lack an indication of extent of probable error. Therefore social statisticians prefer interval estimates stipulating upper and lower limits (as 14 and 10 in this example).

These limits are customarily determined so that, according to the laws of probability, the odds are 95 per cent that the interval includes the true answer and only 5 per cent that the true answer falls outside the band. We speak of these odds as the 95 per cent confidence level; the estimation band is the 95 per cent confidence interval. The term "significance level" is used to designate the probability that the point estimate differs from the true value by a specified amount (in this example, more than two children). Ordinarily the significance level is fixed at a probability of 5 per cent.

Thus there are two interrelated concepts: the estimation interval (bounded by confidence limits) and the confidence level (with its converse, the significance level). The two vary together: the smaller the interval, the less the confidence; the larger the interval, the greater the confidence. Researchers choose willy-nilly between a precise statement (that is, narrow limits) in which they place little confidence, or an imprecise statement (wide limits) in which they repose considerable confidence. Consider for example, a sample survey of opinion concerning eating pizza with anchovies: the survey research team may report odds of 10-to-1 that the American people believe that eating pizza results in indigestion 9 to 21 per cent of the time, or they may record odds of 50-to-1 that Americans claim that indigestion will follow 5 to 26 per cent of such indulgences. (Or, if the investigators are experienced sociologists, they may suspect that gastric disturbances are influenced largely by the diner's convictions or prejudices concerning digestibility—a view that encouraged one dietician to intone, "People can eat and digest anything they really like."). Most difficulties in this statistical decision are illusory, since the subject matter and context generally discourage one alternative.

Ideally sociologists prefer to have the interval small and the confidence level high, but such a "winning combination" is impossible without making the sample very large. Ordinarily researchers are compelled to compromise on a high confidence level for a large estimation interval, a low confidence level for a narrow interval of estimation, or whatever other combination is most consonant with the objectives and uses of the study. It must be understood, however, that none of these choices is possible unless a probability sample is obtained.

By taking a sufficiently large sample, statisticians can

achieve any desired precision and confidence level.[11] This comforting though expensive resolution to estimation tribulations arises from the law of large numbers and the central limit theorem. The Swiss mathematician Jacob Bernoulli's law of large numbers, dating back to 1713, states that the probability that the mean of a sample will differ numerically by more than a given amount from the mean of the universe can be made as small as one wishes by making the sample size sufficiently large. The central limit theorem, first proved by the French mathematician Abraham De Moivre in 1733, states this relation more precisely; the twentieth-century formulation of the theorem specifies a formula for computing the variation in the sampling distribution. Thus the central limit theorem makes possible an accurate and reliable inductive leap from sample to universe. "It is the most important theorem in statistics from both the theoretical and applied points of view."[12]

Hypothesis Testing

In addition to setting confidence limits and levels, social statisticians test hypotheses. To learn, for example, whether atheists or believers in God are better students, sociologists would test the null hypothesis: atheists and believers have identical grade point averages. After conducting a sample survey, the investigators would estimate the mean grade point averages of the two groups. Standard statistical procedures and formulas enable scholars to determine objectively whether to reject or to accept this null hypothesis. Or, instead of considering only the means, they may tabulate the grade point distributions of all atheists and all believers in adjacent columns and evaluate the similarity between the atheist and believer grade distributions.

Statisticians also test hypotheses involving two variables when both are quantitative. In 1952, English

physicians collected a stratified sample of 2,930 persons
to examine the relation between cigarette smoking and
carcinoma of the lung. They found that differences in
proportions of people afflicted by lung cancer between
smokers and nonsmokers and between heavy and light
smokers were beyond the 5 per cent significance level
among women and exceeded the ten-thousandth of 1
per cent level among men. Such a result means that
the chances that the observed differences were attributable to sampling variability (and hence causally neg-
ligible) were 5 per cent for women and infinitesimal
for men.[13]

Hedging conclusions by estimating the ever-present
though sometimes very small uncertainty (as among
the male smokers) is inherent in inference of any kind,
including statistical inference. Scrupulous evaluation
of degree of sureness is the distinguishing mark of the
modern social statistician. Certainly sociological judgments are more realistic and far more valuable when
they do incorporate explicit measures of the likelihood of errors. Statements of uncertainty permit the
appliers of research findings and the makers of policy
to judge for themselves how far to trust the conclusions
and implications of sociological research.

Nonparametric Measures

In the last two decades, social scientists have been
attracted to nonparametric or distribution-free tests—
that is, tests which specify few or no conditions or
parameters or moments of the parent population.[14]
Since sociologists frequently do not know much about
the population (which may be why they are doing the
research in the first place), nonparametric measures
are appealing. Moreover, they are applicable in a
wider variety of circumstances than are the traditional,
parametric measures. However, the parametric tests
are the more powerful and therefore are preferred in
cases where the necessary assumptions are met—specif-

ically, where the values of two or more moments are ascertainable.

Aside from assumptions concerning properties of the parent distribution, another weakness sometimes present in social statistics is the assumption that all variables under examination are independent of each other. Sociological variables, however, are usually not independent. Therefore increasing attention is being devoted to developing and applying such devices as stochastic processes and Markov chains, which do not assume such independence.[15]

To sum up, statistics, whether descriptive (as described in the first two-thirds of this chapter) or inductive (as in the last third), does play an indispensable role in analyzing the characteristics of collected data and drawing inferences therefrom. It is for this reason that sociologists and other social scientists are expected and even required to learn the rudiments of statistics as a part of their academic training. It is again for this reason that sociologists who show evidence of ability to "live with" statistics and to think in statistical lines are rewarded and occasionally even revered, while their statistically obtuse contemporaries are shunted into the background. Indeed, this respect for quantitative manipulation of observed data is coming to be pervasive in sociology.

VI

〜

Computers and Models

＊

If sociology is young, the development of high-powered electronic computers is still more recent. Early in the twentieth century, sociologists came to use and even to assist in developing descriptive and inductive statistics. Today, sociologists are joining other scholars in making use of the computing equipment designed and built since World War II.

Prior to the turn of the century, quantitative skills for data analysis were embarrassingly naïve by modern standards. In part, the recency of mathematical approaches to social phenomena may be attributed to the astonishingly rudimentary methods of counting and computing from antiquity through the Middle Ages and even into the nineteenth century. Of the three R's, 'rithmetic certainly came hardest to man.

Arithmetic

Until Leonardo Fibonacci da Pisa introduced the Arabic system of numeration (borrowed from the Hindus) to Europe in 1202, the four fundamental

arithmetical processes of addition, subtraction, multiplication, and division were performed in incredibly
tedious ways. Multiplication was regarded as extremely
difficult and division was considered a feat that could
be performed only by trained mathematicians.[1] Dantzig tells the story, "characteristic of the situation then
existing," of the fifteenth-century German merchant
who wanted to give his son an advanced commercial
education. Appealing to a university professor, he was
told in all seriousness that adequate instruction in addition and subtraction could be obtained in a German
university, but that the "advanced" arts of multiplying
and dividing could be mastered only in Italy.[2] The
following example provides an insight into the status
of reckoning in the thirteenth century:

THIRTEENTH CENTURY:	TWENTIETH CENTURY:
$27 \times 2 = 54$	27
$27 \times 4 = 54 \times 2 = 108$	$\times 13$
$27 \times 8 = 108 \times 2 = 216$	81
$27 \times 13 = 216 + 108 + 27 = 351$	27
	351

Imagine multiplying 6357 times 847 this way; one
might as well use Roman numerals. This process of
multiplying by doubling was called duplation. Division was performed by mediation or halving. Similarly
cumbersome methods were used in India and other
regions.[3] Even today many people still do not understand how to use the decimal system.

The base 10 was not the unanimous choice that one
might suppose. In fact, it is not yet fully accepted in
the English-speaking world. Americans and English-
men refuse to abandon the cumbersome system of
measurement founded on bases of 3 (feet to a yard),
12 (inches to a foot), 4 (quarts to a gallon), 16
(ounces to a pound), 8 (furlongs to a mile), 5½ (yards
to a rod), 20 (hundred-weights to a ton, grains to a

scruple), 80 (chains to a mile), 60 (minutes to an hour), 14 (pounds to a stone), and some weird fractional combinations. In the metric system of weights and measures, however, all of the comparable numbers are 10 or multiples thereof. Authorities have suggested and used the quinary system (base 5); the vigesimal system (base 20), which left its heritage in "threescore" and "quatre-vingt"; the binary system (base 2), beloved by Leibnitz and now immersed in the entrails of high-speed computers; various prime-based systems (7, 11, and the like) for mathematical irreducibility and the lessening of ambiguity; the sexagesimal system (base 60), used by ancient Chinese and Sumerians; and the duodecimal system (base 12), vigorously advanced by Buffon and responsible for the break in English cardinal numerals between twelve and the 'teens (the Duodecimal Society of America is still trying to replace our "absurd tens" with "sensible twelves"). "That mankind adopted the decimal system is a physiological accident. Those who see the hand [five-fingered?] of Providence in everything will have to admit that providence is a poor mathematician. For outside its physiological merit the decimal base has little to commend itself. Almost any other base . . . would have done as well and probably better."[4]

Even these meager skills were slow in coming. The ancient Sumerians of 4,000 years ago left three legacies that were not sufficiently appreciated by posterity: positional notation (but without zero), negative numbers, and a proto-decimal system.[5] The modern decimal point was foreshadowed by Simon Stevin in 1585 and Franciscus Vieta in 1600 and may have been invented by Bartholomaus Pitiscus in 1608.

Ability to count and manipulate quantities symbolically is a fairly recent accomplishment. Generally men reckoned and calculated through physical manipulation of *calculi* (pebbles in Latin) or other improvements upon the finger. The tally stick and counting board (the prototype of the modern computing aba-

cus) were universal in both the Occident and the
Orient. Not until 1826 did bookkeepers of the English
Court of Exchequer abandon the practice of keeping
accounts on notched elm sticks called tallies, of which
the modern pencil tally by fives and tens is a cousin.
Charles Dickens attributed the burning of the House
of Lords and the House of Commons in 1834 to an
overly ambitious stoking of a stove with an accumulation of obsolete wooden tallies.

Analog Computers

Arithmetic operations and record-keeping are now
coming increasingly to be performed on calculating
machines. Computers are of two basic types: analog
and digital. Analog machines represent numbers by
some analogous quantity, such as length or electric
charge; essentially they are physical models comprised
of measurable quantities. Digital computers count but
do not measure; they represent information by strings
of digits and perform calculations by combining these
numerals. In sum, analog computers measure; digital
computers count.

The earliest computers were of the analog variety.
One of the first, and still probably the most widely
used in the Western world, is the logarithmic slide rule.
Scottish laird John Napier invented logarithms in 1594
and later devised a set of bone or ivory rods which
came to be widely used for multiplication, division,
and the extraction of square and cube roots. Henry
Briggs introduced the decimal base and laboriously
computed tables for publication in 1617. In 1630 William Oughtred invented the slide rule by placing two
logarithmic scales next to each other and allowing one
to move, but it was sparingly used until John Robertson manufactured a 30-inch rule with twelve scales
and a movable hairline. Circular and spiral slide rules
were known in the seventeenth century; in 1881 Edwin
Thatcher developed a cylindrical form. The modern

log-log duplex decitrig slide rule is essentially that designed by French artillery Lieutenant Amédée Mannheim in 1859.[6]

The crucial element of the slide rule is the representation of quantities by length, but with the scale so defined that adding two lengths produces the same result as multiplying together the two original numbers. Division is performed by subtracting one length from the other. Thus a difficult operation (multiplication or division) is converted into an easy one (addition or subtraction). This would be impossible with linear representation of numbers by length; Napier's great contribution was the discovery that a logarithmic analog would permit multiplication to be treated as if it were addition, and division as if it were subtraction.

Other early mechanical calculators constructed by Blaise Pascal in 1642, Samuel Morland in 1666, and Gottfried Wilhelm von Leibnitz in 1694 were primarily adding machines.[7] Multiplication and division, performed by turning cranks and dials operating interlocking wheels, became possible in the eighteenth century.[8]

The pinnacle of mechanical computing was reached in the machines designed and built by Vannevar Bush at the Massachusetts Institute of Technology in 1925-1942 and Howard Aiken at Harvard University in 1937-1944. Such machines were instructed sometimes by means of punched cards developed by Herman Hollerith for the 1890 United States census and sometimes by punched paper tape similar to music rolls for player pianos.

Bush's calculator was fundamentally mechanical, though the basic operation, the rotation of gears through specified angles, was powered by electric motors. Aiken's Mark I was electro-mechanical; the basic operations were performed by mechanical components called relays controlled electrically. The first completely electric computer, the ENAIC, was constructed at the University of Pennsylvania in 1944-1946 by John W. Mauchly and J. Presper Eckert. ENAIC, using vacuum tubes instead of relays or other mechanical devices, was a digital computer.

Digital Computers

Analog computers are limited by the precision with which length, voltage, and other physical quantities can be measured. For this and other reasons, digital computers are now in the ascendant, with analog calculators being confined to certain special-purpose tasks to which they are particularly well fitted. The digital computer offers the advantages of being generally faster, more accurate, physically smaller, and more adaptable to a variety of uses.

The oldest digital computer is the abacus, which has been traced back to 450 B.C. and is still the most widely used calculator in the world. Abacuses have been used by the Greeks, Romans, Hindus, Chinese, and Russians. Consisting of a frame containing beads strung in several rows on wires permitting back-and-forth movement, the abacus is easily learned and enormously quick, but limited in accuracy.

Unquestionably the greatest single contribution to the maturation of computers was made by the English mathematician, Charles Babbage.[9] A full century ahead of his time, Babbage completed a Difference Engine in 1822, which was basically an adding machine containing hundreds of gears, shafts, and ratchets permitting six-place accuracy. In 1833 he conceived a more elaborate idea, the Analytic Engine, which would be able to store 1,000 fifty-digit numbers in several tons of assembled gears and levers sufficiently complex to perform any finite arithmetical operation at a speed of about sixty additions a minute. Unfortunately, however, Babbage's profound conceptual advance demanded more sophisticated metallurgical and other engineering skills than were possessed by contemporary technicians. Consequently the machine was never built, though the inventor sunk into its construction his large personal fortune and considerable funds supplied by the English government. In the Analytic Engine, Babbage proposed to adapt the punched cards invented in 1801 by the Frenchman Joseph M. Jacquard to automate looms for weaving. With patterns of holes representing numerical quantities, the Engine was intended to weave algebraic patterns and complete computations far exceeding its predecessors in complexity, speed, and accuracy.[10] But Babbage's dream had to await improvements in machine-tool and electrical technology.

Some years after Babbage's death in 1871, his imposing dream came true with the construction of ENIAC in 1946, EDVAC (the first computer to store its program internally) in 1949, UNIVAC I (the first commercial computer) in 1951, the IBM 701 (the first really high-speed commercial computer) in 1953, and a host of newer machines, notably the IBM 7090. Today there are more than 25,000 computers in service. And every year they become more numerous, faster, more compact, higher in capacity, more reliable, and more flexible. The upper limit is very high: a universal Turing machine (any general-purpose digital computer) can be constructed, if sufficiently complex, to perform any calculation or symbol-manipulation process that could possibly be performed by any other finite procedure.[11]

Modern Data Processing

All in all, as the preceding section illustrates, we have come a long way from the tally stick. H. G. Wells' futuristic statement of 1903 has indeed turned out to be an accurate prediction of the present: "The time may not be very remote when it will be understood that for complete initiation as an efficient citizen of the new great complex world wide states that are now developing, it is as necessary to be able to compute, to think in averages and maxima and minima, as it is now to be able to read and write."[12] In the words of Lancelot Hogben, "we have all learned to talk in size language."

Today the computers are taking over. Teenagers can buy an electronic brain construction kit for $19.95 while awaiting the moment when they can afford a larger kit at $199.95 or $945.00. Commercial computers such as the widely prevalent IBM 650 are considerably more expensive.

Because computers are almost unbelievably fast—high-speed machines can perform 200,000 operations per second—and because they can manipulate complicated mathematical formulas, they are commonly regarded as "giant superbrains" whose intellects dwarf man's small brain with their higher "think power." A more realistic attitude is to regard computers as "giant superclerks" unsurpassed at accurate and rapid performance of repeated tasks but cumbersome and inefficient—even inaccurate—at one-time-only calculations. Computers are also massive filing cabinets from which stored information can be retrieved in a few seconds. Once a research scholar learns how to translate his instructions into a language that the machine can "read," he can direct its actions in much the same manner as he would supervise a staff of statistical clerks—though of course the machine's results are far more impressive as they are printed out at 1,000 lines a minute. "A computer by itself can do nothing, but the same computer with suitable instructions can solve equations, keep books, list stimuli, predict the weather, or prove theorems in plane geometry."[13] Computers are and seem likely to remain servants rather than masters.

The deception that the reverse is so, arises from the assumption that because computers are faster than people, they are more intelligent. (The time unit employed in assessing modern computers is the microsecond—a millionth of a second.) The falsity of this assumption becomes evident upon reflecting analogously that profound thoughts are not particularly likely to be originated by persons whose speech flows with quicksilver rapidity. That machines do operate so fast as to require a minuscule unit of time to measure their movement is disheartening and demoralizing to opponents of automation, but pro-people enthusiasts might take heart from the knowledge that in a literal sense all the computers can do is add. In computer terms, addition is "pure addition," subtraction is "complementary addition," multiplication is serial pure addition, division is serial complementary addition, and so forth. In fairness, however, it must be acknowledged that computers do add with incredible speed; even though they do multiplication problems by laboriously adding and adding and adding, they are still far faster than human beings using less rudimentary procedures. Nonetheless, we must remember that these machines are ordered by human supervisors to do what they direct, when they direct, and how they direct.

How Computers Work

Computers have five components: input, storage, processing, output, and control. Input, the transference of information into the machine, takes place through punched cards, punched paper tape, magnetic tape, or magnetic ink (as on checks). The storage unit is the machine's memory, in which information can be held indefinitely awaiting processing instructions. The processing or arithmetic or logic unit performs various operations upon the stored data; here are the gears, relays, tubes, or transistors (Babbage called this the "mill") that manipulate the data. Output is the display of results, usually in typed form. The control unit coordinates or programs the other units so that the specified operations are performed in the desired sequence. Not all of these units are equally fast; although processing takes place at phenomenal speeds, the over-all speed of computers is restricted to that of their slowest components—input and output.

Input is most commonly achieved through the IBM cards now so familiar to employees of huge companies and to students registering at large universities. An IBM card contains eighty columns, each having twelve rows. By punching rectangular holes into a column, the operator may record any digit from zero to nine, plus two "zonal" punches which, when combined with the ten digital punches, may designate a total of up to thirty categories in a single column. In this fashion an eighty-column card may convey a remarkable quantity of information—and if that does not suffice, additional cards are used. In a typical IBM operation, clerks punch information into these eighty-column cards, using one card (or a set of cards) for each respondent, subject, or family. The cards then may be run through a sorting machine to ascertain the frequency distribution for every variable (ordinarily one column represents a variable), or the information contained on the cards may be put into the memory or storage unit of a machine in readiness for subsequent processing and eventual printing out of results.

Some machines can "read" and, depending on how one defines the word, "learn."[14] The perceptron constructed at Cornell University by Frank Rosenblatt can make visual discriminations between words. The Raytheon Company's Cybertron recognizes sounds. RAND Corporation's JOHNNIAC, named for John von Neumann, one of the leading figures in computer development, can prove theorems and plays a respectable game of chess; the IBM 704 plays checkers and learns how to improve its playing. Since computers boast these and other accomplishments, some humans believe that machines can think and possess intelligence. Others contend that computers are nothing more than *idiots savants* or morons capable of performing certain difficult tasks at spectacular rates but incapable of true thought. When one day psychologists agree on what intelligence is and how thinking takes place, we shall perhaps be able to answer the perplexing, humbling, and now meaningless questions: "Can computers think?" and "Are machines intelligent?" In the meantime, researchers are concentrating on optimum ways to use the known powers of these superclerks of doubtful intelligence.

Since computers are superlatively rapid at processing and abundantly capable at storage but relatively slow at input and output, it follows that wise use of them calls for scheduling as much work as possible on the memory and arithmetic units and as little as can be managed on input and output. As of now, calculations involving a great deal of planning and little actual calculating may be performed more efficiently on a desk calculator, especially in view of the high rental fees of IBM equipment. At the not unusual rental of $500 an hour, wasting ten minutes of machine time (during which a computer might do as many calculations as a man working an eight-hour day could produce in a decade) to mull over a problem and convey it to the machine (which for a human being is remarkably rapid thinking and programming) constitutes profligate squandering of company money. On the other hand, data manipulation requiring lengthy series of calculations and relatively little organizing and assembling is ideally suited to computers. Moreover, the more times a set of material is processed, the greater the relative advantage of the computer over manual or semi-manual procedures such as desk calculators. Underlying both considerations is the machine's demand for absolutely precise data and instructions, with the corollaries that data always need to be "cleaned up" (computer slang for weeding out inconsistencies, incompleteness, and other forms of sloppiness that become more noticeable when cast before data processing equipment), and that programs of computer instructions must be "debugged" (computerese for removal of mistakes from programs and malfunctions from machines). The greater the operational repetitiveness, the less time is taken up in these frustrating but essential bits of preparation for input. An instance of an eminently computerizable type of work is a series of interview surveys repeated monthly and always using the same sample design; another, the weekly payroll of a business firm. In sum, the computer's forte is repetition —extremely rapidly and on a vast scale.

Programming

When punched cards, magnetic tape, or other devices are used to instruct a machine on how to proceed, computer operators call the process programming. Instead of intervening physically at each stage of the operations, the programmer prepares a sequence of coded instructions, called a routine, to be followed by the machine. A group of operations is called a subroutine. Graphic or schematic representation of routines and subroutines showing electrical circuitary or logical arrangements within the computer are called flow charts or block diagrams, because they consist of boxes connected by lines and arrows. Repeated operations are indicated by specifying repetitions of subroutines called iterations or loops. Programming can even include provisional instructions—that is, the machine is given procedures for making a decision, and the instructions specify what is to be done following each possible outcome of the decision.

Computers respond to orders much more literally than do human clerks. To a computer, each instruction is a command to perform a certain operation on stored data. Since the repertoire of any computer consists of a set of exceedingly elementary operations, it is necessary for the programmer to supply a minutely detailed list of extremely specific instructions (though the newest machines can accept somewhat abbreviated commands). Provided these orders are unambiguous, the computer follows them exactly and undeviatingly. However, since the machine does precisely and relentlessly what it is told to do, without using the common sense sometimes exhibited by human clerks, the programmer must anticipate all contingencies at each step. For example, men can understand messages like "Mery Christmas," but most machines take the misspelling literally and are nonplussed by such spurious information. Hence the necessity to debug, which consists largely of finding and correcting human mistakes that would not perturb other humans but which render machines helpless or, worse, cause them to operate incorrectly. In fact, debugging generally takes far more time than computing itself; there may be six or eight debugging runs in preparation for the single, final "true" run.

It frequently happens that a user of a computer needs precisely the same program as a previous user. Recognition of this circumstance has led to establishment of libraries of programs in computing laboratories. Thus a sociologist who needs to calculate a batch of Pearsonian r's or chi-squares has only to locate an existing library program; he need not face the tedium of writing out and debugging the desired program anew each time a computer is used.

Programming or talking to computers is facilitated by several programming languages, of which the most useful to sociologists is called FORTRAN, an acronym for Formula Translator. Similar languages have been developed for business and other uses. Most of these languages can be learned in a week of intensive study.

Today, as has been indicated, computers must be ordered about like menials. But computer technicians are not satisfied with this relationship, and the newest computer development emphasizes designing cleverer computers, with which researchers may carry on give-and-take communication instead of dispensing peremptory commands. In a few years man-machine collaboration promises a spectacular and self-accelerating payoff as both machines and men contribute to further advances.

Binary Bits and Information

Exploitation of the powers of computers depends on one's ability to put information into them—to talk their language. The language or algebra of digital computers is binary. All digital computers use binary or two-valued digits rather than decimal or ten-valued digits to represent stored data. A binary digit, known as a bit (from BInary digiT), has only two values: yes or no, on or off, or, in customary computer terminology, o or 1.[15] Binary digits have the advantage of electrical simplicity: a switch is closed or open; a circuit is conducting or not conducting current. Although the simplicity of the binary system makes it seem on first inspection highly inappropriate as a basis for high-powered, ultra-swift modern computers, it is actually the best system to use—though it took some years to convince engineers of this paradoxical fact. The "on-off" quality of the binary system makes slight demands on electrical circuitry, whereas a higher-valued system requires relatively minute discrimination, which results in larger, slower, and more costly equipment.

Conveying information to a computer is equivalent to designating one out of a number of possible choices. By thus ruling out certain choices, uncertainty or ambiguity is reduced. In the binary system one possibility out of two is specified: married, "1", or single, "0"; alive or dead; male or female. In the case of more sophisticated variables, two or more bits may be required; for example, "00" may signify "single, never married," and "01" "single, previously married." This process may be carried as far as needed: "011" may designate "single, previously married, divorced," whereas "010" indicates "single, previously married, widowed." A fourth bit could identify the means whereby divorce was obtained or the circumstances under which widowhood occurred.

The quantity of information conveyed is measured

by the number of bits required to isolate the given choice or category. A typical computer may have a memory capacity of, say, four million bits, which is roughly equivalent in quantity of information to this book. Additionally, external memories (magnetic tapes or metal disks) may store another billion bits that are accessible indirectly (and therefore relatively slowly) to the computer. The study of sequences of choices from among fixed numbers of bits or alternatives is known as information theory.

Behavior Units

Computer analysis and information theory share with functional analysis and other aspects of sociology the need for an elementary particle—that is, a minimum unit of observation. In all scientific fields, the search for elementary particles is a significant and continuing part of research, as is illustrated by the discovery in physical science of molecules, then atoms, then electrons, and next, hopefully, an elementary unit that will dissipate the chaos presently attendant upon use of several dozen subatomic entities.

"The smallest observable meaningful manifestation of a living organism" is called a behavior item.[16] By "reducing" social behavior into such items and clusters thereof, the sociologist is able to state precisely what he is talking about—an essential step toward scientific objectivity and precision. An example of a behavior unit is a child stretching his arm and hand toward a piece of candy. A behavior cluster includes several component items: reaching for the candy, grasping it, conveying it to his mouth, putting it in his mouth, masticating it, swallowing it, and smiling in pleasure. The set of items clustered together supplies context, meaning, and purpose. Translation of theories into such elementary, minuscule terms of behavior renders them accessible to pointed, detailed testing.

Simulation of Social Behavior

Use of the behavior item also facilitates computer simulation of social behavior, by which is meant setting up a machine reproduction of a real-life social situation so that the investigator may observe the working out of behavior as various stimuli are presented. Machine simulation is now the vogue in many intellectual areas. And even business and industrial concerns are enthusiastic about its performance and potentialities.

Broadly defined, simulation is nothing new; people have been setting up and operating physical models and paper replications of reality for many years. Testing scale models of boats in laboratory tanks is a form of physical simulation. On paper, scientists work out formulas and blueprints to estimate what will happen to a new product or process. In everyday life a family budget simulates expenditures, and an individual can program an anticipated action and its correlative expense into the budget to preview its effect on family solvency without incurring the risk of actually buying the commodity under examination.

Computer simulation is essentially similar, though it can handle far more variables over a longer time period with greater accuracy. Because of its greater complexity, computer simulation is more than just a fancy title; it designates a "dry run" that would require thousands or even millions of man-hours and dollars— an extravagance of human and financial resources that no pre-computer system could afford. Simulation is used in many fields: psychology (the Perceptron's representation of a neural network to identify letters of the alphabet), space research (a trip to Venus by the Jet Propulsion Laboratories of the California Institute of Technology), economic geography (Pakistan's Indus River Valley irrigation system), physiology (the human nervous system), linguistics (machines which partially cope with grammatical irregularities and idio-

matic peculiarities), education (B. F. Skinner's teaching machines and the derivative programmed self-
instruction textbooks), physics (energy generated and
stored in a nuclear reactor), industry (steel mills
and highway bridges), political science (business firms
and international systems), and sociology (interaction
in small groups and large bureaucracies).

Construction and manipulation of an operating
model of a social system or process enable the researcher to by-pass some of the more distressing
disadvantages of the real world. Certain states of considerable theoretical interest occur rarely, and when
they do happen, they may be obscured by other more
prominent but less interesting forces. Social scientists
cannot freely manipulate time, national policies, or
community actions. But through simulation, an experimenter can compress or expand time, artificially dupli-
cating the operations of a social organization over
several years in a manner of minutes; he can simulate
two nations identical except in one respect, thus providing the control group so valuable to causal inference
but never found in real life; he can repeat a given
situation many times, each with a slight modification of
parameters, noting differences in outcomes as the conditions change one variable at a time. In sum, the investigator can become an experimenter because simulation enables him to exercise an unprecedented
amount of control over complex situations.

The dominating requirement and most important
problem inhering in simulation is adequate replication
of the real system. The simulated model must reproduce closely the relevant attributes of the social structure it purports to represent; otherwise the results of
experimentation will be invalidated. But with knowledge and care, "states may be created, reasonably exact
replicates ensured, necessary contrasts obtained, confounding factors randomized, extraneous disturbances
eliminated, and the processes observed comprehen-

sively, precisely, and more or less at the will of the investigator."[17]

One of the virtues of computer simulation is that the computer is a hard master, forcing the researcher to be specific and exact concerning the variables he uses and the relations between them. Another virtue lies in the computer's ability to consider simultaneously and systematically far more variables and interrelationships than any one individual or research team could hope to handle without electronic assistance.

Treating each behavior item as a bit or group of bits is a first step toward machine programming. Once complex group and individual behavior is broken up into clearly defined segments, it may be simulated on computers, thus contributing to comprehension and presumably in the end to increased ability to predict social behavior. In this fashion "it becomes possible to make real predictions in real time about social interaction in small groups."[18] A recent instance is the computer model of five propositions taken from George C. Homans' *Social Behavior* by sociologists at System Development Corporation.[19] Analog and digital simulation, now being undertaken cautiously and for the first time, is another among the many evidences of increased adoption of scientific instruments in studying people in groups.

Mathematical Models

Simulation is part of the recent trend toward development of closed logical systems and empirical equations of sufficient intricacy and rigor to be referred to as mathematical models. Physicist Willard Gibbs said that "mathematics is a language," and statistical pioneer Karl Pearson entitled his masterwork *The Grammar of Science*. This language is not only quantitative but includes all forms of logical reasoning; hence, any meaningful proposition can be phrased in mathematical form.

Models have three connotations. They may represent states, objects, and events in much the same sense in which an architect constructs a small-scale model of a building. They may imply a degree of perfection or idealization, as in a model student or a model husband. Or they may demonstrate how something works. Generally models are less complicated than reality and hence lead more directly to causal generalizations. They are also easier to manipulate and transport than the real thing.[20]

In the world of the model, only the relevant properties of reality are included; for example, in a model of interpersonal relations within a crew of workmen, color of hair and conformation of feet may be omitted because they are presumed to be irrelevant to group relations. Sociological models, like other mathematical models, are selected sets of statements about reality in a given situation; selection ordinarily proceeds on the basis of variables identified in Chapter I. Hardly ever do models attempt to encompass all possible variables. For instance, one model attempting to explain migratory behavior uses one dependent and seven independent variables; a complete explanation of human migration would probably demand dozens of additional independent variables.[21]

Models offer both direct and indirect benefits. They contribute to understanding by organizing data into coherent systems. They provide incentives for data-collecting agencies to improve accuracy. They test old theories and suggest new ones. If successful, they explain interrelationships between independent and dependent variables and ultimately lend themselves to prediction. As Herbert Simon has noted: "Formalization of the systems in which highly rational and individualistic behavior is postulated has already reached a point of development where mathematical theory is displacing literary theory on the frontiers of research."[22]

Mathematical models of human behavior have been advanced by a substantial number of scholars, including psychologists, economists, and mathematicians in addition to sociologists. The most prominent models have been contributed by Rashevsky,[23] Dodd,[24] and von Neumann and Morgenstern.[25] Also noteworthy are the models of Robert R. Bush, William K. Estes, Paul F. Lazarsfeld, Frederick Mosteller, Lewis F. Richardson, Kenneth E. Boulding, George K. Zipf, Norbert Wiener, and Samuel A. Stouffer, examining such diverse subjects as human learning, attitudes, migration, war, and personal interaction.

Operations Research

When a mathematical model reduces a social or technical process to mathematical form in order to facilitate decision-making, the analysis is known as operations research. O.R. is a technique for making explicit and therefore eventually more reliable or efficient the procedures through which a given outcome (such as an industrial product or a military victory) is achieved. Its development since World War II has been rapid and effective. Implemented by the electronic computer, O.R. promises to save many man-hours and thereby ensure greater efficiency of business and administrative activity.

Shortly before the Second World War a new idea began to emerge—the concept of statistical decision. This new concept is founded on probability, statistical inference, information theory, and mathematical models. Statistical decision can be viewed as a complex machine into which is fed information from the real world, and out of which comes a recommendation for action in that world. Yet the fundamental mechanics of the machine are symbolic: the practical problem is translated into symbolic language, the problem is solved in symbolic form, and the solution is then translated back into practical terms as a decision.[26]

Operations research is an application of statistical decision, which in turn is based on a probabilistic approach to scientific method. The major phases of O.R. are formulating the problem, constructing a mathematical model to represent the system being studied, deriving a symbolic solution for the model, testing the model and solution, and implementing or putting to work the solution thus verified.[27]

Decision-Making

The decision-making facet of research methodology is frequently overlooked by the novice or outsider in his assumption that model builders and methodologists are put on earth to solve certain technical problems in purely mechanical ways. Statisticians are accustomed to being accosted by statistically unlettered scholars with requests for a quantitative technique that will apply universally to all items in a questionnaire—or for a single measure that will always perform a certain statistical trick. The nonstatistician is first surprised and then bored and finally exasperated by the statistician's seemingly unnecessary curiosity about the manner of securing the data, evidence from analogous studies, and the use to be made of the conclusions. But what the lay scholar attributes to fussiness or impertinence or obstructiveness is a necessary part of the decision-making process. The statistician must inform himself of the assumptions and characteristics underlying the data he confronts—such as level of measurement, form of distribution, and type of sample —because it is precisely such knowledge that is prerequisite to selecting the most appropriate statistical measure. For example, in computing averages, the statistician must decide whether to apply the mode, median, mean, or another measure of central tendency. If an inappropriate measure is selected, computation however accurately performed will proceed in a wrong direction, and subsequent interpretation of results will suffer to the extent of being grossly misleading or even contradictory to an interpretation based upon legitimate methodological operations. Using the mean where the median is called for may result from intent to deceive or from simple ignorance; in either case, the results can be disastrous to accurate understanding of the observed data.

The importance of decision-making in social research may be seen in a common personnel arrangement. Let us consider, for example, a research group (composed of, say, a director, his assistant, and a dozen interviewers, coders, and clerks) which approaches a methodologist and a statistician for consulting purposes. The methodological consultant does not actually interview anyone; nor does the statistical consultant do any computing. Both experts do ascertain, however, what has gone before and make decisions regarding interviewing procedures, question construction and sequence, IBM card punching, statistical description, hypothesis testing, and related concerns. The project director then assigns to his interviewers and statistical clerks the job of carrying out these directives. The consultants would be bored by undertaking these operations, and their higher fees might bankrupt the project were they to perform such front-line tasks. The major reason why the consultants demand and receive hourly remuneration amounting to several times that of the other workers is that they possess knowledge of the techniques of research, enough experience to anticipate how each given technique might work out in the stated situation, and the intelligence to apply this training efficiently and accurately. In short, they are paid to decide what others can merely guess.

Example: Civil Liberties

*

Readers who have faithfully followed the methodological discussions of Chapters II through VI may be curious as to how these research operations work when attacking a specific problem. This chapter describes a "real life" study making use of many of the foregoing techniques.

Of course, no one research study uses all of the principles and techniques outlined in the preceding four chapters, though most field research does utilize a large portion of the total methodological skills. Nonetheless a social researcher must know enough about each technique so as to decide whether or not to apply it to his project. Further, if he does decide on a given set of research operations, he must be capable of respecting their intricacies and shortcomings.

Stouffer's Survey

Surely one of the most capable decision-makers in sociological research has been the late Samuel A. Stouffer of Harvard University. Prompted by concern over the hysterical reactions of many Americans in the 1950's, including members of the United States Senate and House of Representatives, to the threat of Communist espionage and sabotage, the Fund for the Republic authorized Stouffer to undertake an opinion survey on this subject by interviewing a cross-section of the American people.[1]

The survey examined in some depth the responses of Americans to danger posed by the Communist conspiracy outside and within the United States and also to that posed by those patriots who choose to thwart the conspiracy by sacrificing certain of America's traditional individual liberties. In May, June, and July 1954, when the inquiry was conducted, no topic was more timely or controversial.

Stouffer's study exemplifies what social research can discover about attitudes of the citizenry toward a theme laden with bitter strife. Some observers contend that scientific research is impossible when one is confronted with subject matter seemingly inseparable from strong feelings and frequently violent discord. Selection of a subject for investigation heavily fraught with emotionality and at the same time so crucial for national policy thus constitutes a severe test of the ability of social researchers to achieve objectivity, especially when, as was the case here, the principal investigator himself held powerful views on the subject.

Theory and Causation

The topicality of Stouffer's research was supplemented by an attempt to relate findings to theory about tolerance and prejudice. Timeliness alone justified this particular study, but the possibility of transience was avoided by establishing theoretical relevance.

Social theorists have postulated, for instance, that education is related to tolerance of political and social nonconformity and also to prejudice toward minority ethnic and religious groups. Higher education appears to generate greater acceptance of and tolerance toward differences stemming from a variety of sources: ideology, race, status and role, or folkways and mores. In the French idiom, to understand is to excuse. Not only do schooling and reading put a person in contact with those whose beliefs and customs differ from his own, but knowledge of variation appears to be a necessary though not sufficient condition for tolerance of disagreement and irregular behavior. When one has met with enough actions and ideas differing from his own, he may gradually lose his repugnance for the strange and his fear of strangers and become receptive to the new and willing to shake hands. Tolerance of deviation seems to demand recognition that difference is not a proof of inferiority or evil.[2]

Another instance of wider import of the study, beyond its immediate concern with political policy, lies in the theory of the authoritarian personality. Relevant to Stouffer's survey—and what is far more important here, partially testable by it—is the thesis that authoritarianism and rigid categorization of experience tend to generate intolerance.[3]

Variables and Hypotheses

Various scholars have also hypothesized as being related to prejudice and attitude toward nonconformity such variables as size of community of residence (metropolis dwellers learn to live with a wide variety of people, whereas farmers and villagers generally meet only their own kind); degree of optimism (frustration and anxiety lead to suspicion and hostility toward others, whereas rosy-colored glasses encourage friendliness and tolerance); migration experience (exposure to a new value system and way of life educates and aids understanding, while always living in the same place makes different ideas seem dangerous); and age (young people are more open-minded and hence more tolerant). Regardless of their degree of plausibility, however, these interconnections between variables need to be examined before being accepted or rejected.

Thus the literature existing prior to 1954 suggested a number of independent variables that might be related to attitudes toward nonconformist behavior. In any research, the investigator can benefit from close reading of the literature, which may suggest how to modify and supplement the researcher's intentions regarding which variables to include in the interview schedule and how to relate them to each other. Awareness of what other scholars have written on the subject is essential to making competent decisions regarding which variables to examine and what hypotheses to test. Moreover, when existing knowledge on the subject is scanty, setting up formal hypotheses for testing may prove impossible or inadvisable. Pioneering studies—called pilot studies—frequently omit hypotheses from their design; an important part of their intent is to learn enough about a new subject to suggest hypotheses to be tested in subsequent research.

Partly because Stouffer was studying a topic about which few hard facts are known (attitude toward civil liberties is a topic characterized by hundreds of soft facts, thousands of firm opinions, and very little solid knowledge) and partly because the published book reporting results was directed at a popular audience which could not be presumed to understand the advantages of null hypotheses, he opened his first chapter with a series of questions, some of which are tantamount to hypotheses. For example:[4]

> Who are the people most likely to have given the sober second thought to the problems with which we are concerned?
> What about the attitudes of responsible civic leaders as compared with the rank and file within a community?
> Are we raising a new generation which will be more

sensitive or less sensitive than its elders to threats to freedom?

Do attitudes differ in different regions of the country? In cities as compared with rural areas? Among men as compared with women? What role does religion play?

How important are agencies of mass communication likely to be in evoking more thoughtful reflection on the issues of Communism and civil liberties?*

Schedule of Questions

Having established the subject, some major queries, and a set of variables to be investigated, Stouffer then prepared questions to be asked by interviewers.[5] In this case, the investigator's decision favored free-answer or open-ended questions, though check-list questions were also included. While recognizing that heavy reliance upon open-ended questions carries the disadvantages of lengthening the interview, depending crucially on the objectivity and accuracy of the interviewer in identifying and recording salient remarks in a lengthy response, and adding monumentally to the job of coding, Stouffer chose this type of question because of its ability to measure the depth and intensity of opinions evoked. Some of the open-ended questions were:

What kinds of things do you worry most about?

Do you think Americans are getting more suspicious of others, or less suspicious? (Probes:) Why do you say this? In what ways?

What kind of people in America are most likely to be Communists? (Probe:) What racial and religious groups are they most likely to be in? (Probe:) What kind of jobs are they most likely to be in?

* Samuel A. Stouffer, *Communism, Conformity, and Civil Liberties.* Copyright © 1955 by Samuel A. Stouffer. Reprinted by permission of Doubleday & Company, Inc.

Some check-response questions were:

In politics today, do you consider yourself a Democrat, Republican, or Independent?

What is your religious preference—Protestant, Catholic, or Jewish? Have you attended church or religious services in the last month?

What is the last grade you finished in school?

In what country were you born?

Are you married, single, widowed, or divorced?

Frequently, Stouffer chose to use a series of questions in preference to a single question to ascertain a given opinion. Two sets of related questions, one comprising fifteen questions and the other nine, were used to form scales.

Five successive versions of the schedule were prepared, pre-tested in interviews, and revised to promote comprehensibility. Approximately three times as many questions were tried out as appeared in the final draft. Yet far from being the waste effort it may appear to the uninformed, such expenditure of time, energy, and money is necessary to the search for an interviewing instrument that will elicit and classify attitudes with discernment and penetration; even the most highly qualified investigators go through this pre-testing process.

The average final interview required an hour and a quarter. Depending on the loquaciousness of the respondent, the extent of his experience, the need for probing, and related factors, interview time ranged from thirty minutes to three hours.

Sample Design

After revisions indicated by pre-testing, the final interview schedule was administered to 6,466 men and women throughout the country by 535 skilled interviewers supplied by the American Institute of Public Opinion and the National Opinion Research Center.

Persons interviewed were selected by sampling experts on the staffs of these two national research agencies. Two samples were taken: a cross-section of 4,933 of the nation's people and a special sample of 1,533 local community leaders.

The cross-section constituted a multi-stage cluster probability sample representative of the United States population 21 years of age and older living in private households (thus excluding inhabitants of hospitals, nursing homes, prisons, hotels, and military camps). First, the states were grouped into 26 regions. Then the state economic areas within each region were clustered into two categories: metropolitan and nonmetropolitan. Next the counties comprising the state economic areas were subdivided into three rural-urban strata: 50,000 and over, 2,500 to 49,999, and smaller than 2,500. From this array of cities and minor civil divisions, ordered alphabetically within strata, the investigators drew a systematic sample, keeping the probability of selection of each place proportionate to its population in the 1950 Census. Within the cities so selected, census tracts and wards were drawn, again keeping the probability of selection proportional to population size; within each tract or ward a block was drawn at random. Those municipalities too small to have tracts or wards were broken down by the researchers into segments so delineated as to be roughly equal in population; segments were then selected randomly. Rural areas were similarly subdivided, with segments also chosen at random. Inside each block or urban segment thus randomly selected, 75 dwelling units were listed beginning from a random starting point; in rural segments, 50 dwelling units were listed in the same manner. The primary sampling units thus consisted of clusters of 75 dwelling units in urban areas and 50 in rural areas. From each primary sampling unit a systematic sample was taken consisting of ten dwelling units. Adults in each occupied dwelling unit drawn into the sample were ordered by age and sex, and final selection of sample members was made randomly. No substitutions were permitted; if the sample member was not contacted on the first visit, interviewers called again until at least five attempts had been made.

The sample of community leaders was independent of the cross-section sample. Unlike the latter, it was not a probability sample and made no pretense of being representative of community leaders throughout the United States. Because of the difficulty of defining and comparing leaders when communities diverge drastically in size, only cities of 10,000 to 150,000 population were included in the sample frame. The randomly chosen areas used in the cross-section sample contained 123 cities of this size, constituting a representative set of all such urban communities in the nation. In each of these cities, interviewers were instructed to identify and interview fourteen uniquely defined community leaders (mayor, Community Chest chairman, publisher of the largest newspaper, chairman of the school board, regent of the D.A.R., commander of the largest American Legion post, and so forth).

Sampling Errors and Bias

The national cross-section, being a probability sample, might be expected to resemble the adult civilian population from which it was drawn. The extent to which the sample reconstructed the national population is illustrated by the following percentages in the nation and the sample, respectively: male, 48 per cent and 47 per cent; Negro, 9 per cent and 9 per cent; high school education, 44 per cent and 45 per cent; aged 60 and older, 20 per cent and 20 per cent; urban, 64 per cent and 66 per cent; southern region, 29 per cent and 31 per cent.[6] The sample appears very similar to the population from which it was taken, thus implying that sampling procedures and nonresponse were probably not biasing.

The 4,933 usable interviews were obtained from an original sample of 5,881, yielding an exceptionally high completion rate of 84 per cent. The 16 per cent "fish which were not caught" were distributed as follows: not at home after five calls, 6 per cent; too sick, 1 per cent; could not speak the language (bilingual interviewers were used in some areas), 1 per cent; refused to be interviewed, 7 per cent; and broke off interview, 1 per cent.[7] Although any loss from a probability sample is a potential source of bias, this 16 per cent loss rate is about as low as can reasonably be expected.

The proportion of completed interviews in the community leader sample was somewhat larger. Of 1,688 leaders identified, 91 per cent yielded completed interviews; 4 per cent were out of town, sick, or otherwise unavailable; 2 per cent could not be contacted; and 3 per cent refused the interview or broke it off after beginning. The percentage of completions was highest among American Legion commanders and exceeded 90 per cent in all but three of the fourteen leader types: labor union leaders (88 per cent), Democratic party county chairmen (87 per cent), and newspaper publishers (80 per cent).[8]

Since no experimental stimulus was introduced, the time span between the earliest (May) and latest (July) interviews was not intended to be meaningful. Differences in responses by four time periods (May 15-31, June 1-15, June 16-30, and July 1-31) were discovered to be insignificant.[9]

Bias attributable to other factors than sampling is more difficult to evaluate. Returns were examined for internal inconsistency and evidences of faulty rapport, and only experienced interviewers were employed. Nonetheless, there remains (as always) a possibility that an unduly high proportion of undetected bias did creep into the completed schedules.

Scale Construction

For economy of presentation as well as reliability, responses to 24 questions were grouped to form two scales: willingness to tolerate nonconformists and perception of internal Communist danger. Let us consider the first as an example of the construction and use of scales.

Degree of willingness to recognize the rights of non-conformists was indicated by fifteen questions arranged into five sets or subtests of three items apiece. From these five subtests were designated six groups of respondents. Those at one extreme tended to be tolerant on all five subtests; those in the second group tended to give tolerant answers to all subtests except the one on which it was hardest to be tolerant; and those in the third group responded tolerantly to four subtests—all but the two hardest ones. At the other extreme were respondents who were tolerant on no subtest, followed by those who were tolerant on only one—the easiest on which to make tolerant replies—and next, those who tended to reply in a tolerant fashion to the two subtests of easiest tolerance but who had intolerant reactions on the other four. Of course, none of the six groups was entirely consistent. The degree of consistency was reflected in the coefficient of reproducibility, which measures the extent to which the respondents achieved regularly patterned scores on the five subtests, permitting scholars to infer from the total score (here, zero through five) how an individual responded to each component subtest contributing to that score. By convention this coefficient must be at least .90 to ensure acceptability of a scale. This method of construction yields a Guttman scale, as described in Chapter IV.

Stouffer found that community leaders are considerably more tolerant of nonconformist behavior than the rank and file respondents in the cross-section, both for the nation and when confined to the same 123 cities. However, American Legion commanders, D.A.R. regents, and women's club presidents fell far lower than other leaders on the relative tolerance scale, scoring only slightly higher in degree of tolerance than the rank and file.[10]

Statistical Description

In addition to scales, a large number of bivariate and trivariate tables and also some bar charts were used in presenting results. The decision to restrict presentation of findings to these rather elementary forms was probably influenced by two factors: the exploratory nature of the study and the orientation of the book toward a popular rather than a professional audience, both of which circumstances generally discourage use of highly sophisticated statistics.

Typical of Stouffer's presentational format is his manner of reporting the impact on the dependent variable, tolerance, of the independent variables, region of residence and size of community. When scale scores for willingness to tolerate nonconformists are tabulated separately for each of four regions of the nation, it is apparent that residents of the West are most tolerant, followed in order by inhabitants of the East, Middle West, and South. Classifying data by four types of community discloses that relative tolerance of nonconformists is highest in metropolitan areas and lower, in order, for other cities, small towns (below 2,500 population), and farms.[11]

Since the lowest levels of tolerance are found in the South and Middle West regions and in rural villages and farms, and since we know that these two regions have higher proportions of rural people than do the more urban West and East, we should inquire whether the regional differences can be accounted for solely by differences in the urban-rural population distribution. This issue may be resolved by cross-tabulating degree of tolerance against both region and urbanization simultaneously, performing multiple and partial correlation analysis, and applying corresponding significance tests. Table 1 reveals that within every one of the four community sizes, Southerners ranked lowest in relative tolerance. Westerners ranked highest in three categories, being barely exceeded by the East

TABLE 1. Willingness to Tolerate Nonconformity by Community Type and Region*

Community type and region	Percentage distribution of relative tolerance scores			Number of cases
	LOW	MEDIUM	HIGH	
Metropolitan areas				
West	12	34	54	282
East	11	42	47	663
Middle West	12	54	34	543
South	23	53	24	403
Other cities				
West	15	39	46	227
East	19	50	31	332
Middle West	17	50	33	406
South	26	58	16	397
Small towns				
West	19	47	34	110
East	16	49	35	223
Middle West	19	54	27	243
South	24	62	14	341
Farms				
West	15	50	35	40
East	25	57	18	44
Middle West	19	55	26	273
South	37	53	10	405

in the small town classification. Thus we may conclude that the presence of a larger proportion of rural people in the South does not explain the region's relative lack of tolerance toward nonconformists. Neither can we erase the influence of regionalism in the West. However, in the other two regions, cross-tabulation presents a more complicated picture. With the exception of metropolitan areas, differences in tolerance scores be-

* Samuel A. Stouffer, *Communism, Conformity, and Civil Liberties,* New York, Doubleday and Co., 1955, pp. 116 and 118.

tween Easterners and Midwesterners are too small to
be significant. In sum, cross-tabulation by a third
variable, community size, refines our understanding of
the relation between regionality and tolerance by ac-
counting for much of the East-Middle West difference
and a small part of the West-other northern distinctions, but the South's low tolerance scores remain even
after introduction of urban-rural classes.

Now let us reinspect the data from another dimension. Can the lower tolerance ratings of villagers and
farmers be explained by the fact that so many of them
are Southerners or Midwesterners? If within each
region, differences in tolerance scores according to
community size tend to vanish, we would conclude
that community type is not as important as region.
Inspection of the table discloses, however, that within
every region, metropolitan dwellers have the highest
tolerance scores, residents of other cities tend to be
intermediate, and farmers and villagers score lowest.
From this analysis we may confidently judge that
urban-rural differences do exist irrespective of region.

Thus both region and community type are discovered to be independently meaningful sources of
differences—or are they explainable by still another
variable? Education seems a likely fourth variable
to consider, for city people generally have more schooling than do rural people, and Northerners tend to be
better educated than Southerners. So we face a new
question: could education explain away the observed
differences in tolerance between North and South, between city and farm?

Subclassification of tolerance scores into five educational levels by region and community is presented in
Table 2; in the interest of simplification, only the high
tolerance percentages are included. Note that four general patterns emerge. First, education is strongly related to tolerance of nonconformity: percentages of
high tolerance scores at the higher educational levels
are nearly always greater than corresponding percent-

TABLE 2. Willingness to Tolerate Nonconformity by Education, Region and Community Type*

Education and region	*Percentage classified as "more tolerant" on scale of tolerance*			
	METRO-POLITAN	OTHER URBAN	VILLAGE	FARM
College graduates				
West	73	84	—	—
East	78	54	—	—
Middle West	64	65	68	—
South	62	45	—	—
Some college				
West	67	69	—	—
East	63	59	—	—
Middle West	59	61	32	52
South	55	21	29	—
High school graduates				
West	57	41	32	—
East	57	41	44	—
Middle West	42	45	29	43
South	26	18	19	15
Some high school				
West	52	40	41	—
East	39	27	26	—
Middle West	31	23	17	13
South	20	23	13	10
Grade school				
West	27	35	18	—
East	27	11	17	—
Middle West	18	18	11	14
South	7	4	6	9

* Samuel A. Stouffer, *Communism, Conformity, and Civil Liberties,* New York, Doubleday and Co., 1955, pp. 120-121. No percentages are shown unless based on 20 or more cases.

ages at lower educational levels. Second, not a single percentage in the South is as high as any corresponding figure in the three northern regions. Obviously amount of education is not responsible for North-South discrepancies. However, well-educated Southerners do show evidence of greater tolerance toward nonconformity than do poorly-educated Northerners. Third, even when education and community size are held constant, the West still appears to have the highest percentage of more tolerant scores. Fourth, metropolitan residents are consistently more tolerant than are village and farm people, but differences between metropolitan and other cities are inconsistent and probably not statistically significant. Thus we conclude that education, region, and community all influence degree of tolerance of nonconformity.

But the analysis is still unfinished. Another explanatory variable that might be considered is race. Stouffer's study found Negroes to be less tolerant than whites, even when subclassified by region. Unfortunately, the size of the sample does not permit simultaneous breakdown by a fifth variable (because the numbers of persons in many of these multi-variate categories or table cells become too small for reliable generalizing), but partial cross-tabulation indicates that Negro-white tolerance differences tend to disappear when education is held constant. Higher order multi-variate analysis was not feasible in this study, though age, sex, church attendance, and other variables were examined in relation to relative tolerance scores.

Significance of Differences

In any sample survey the question arises as to how large differences need to be to become statistically significant. If a sample is small, differences of 10 or even 20 per cent may not be statistically significant at the 95 per cent level; in small numbers there is no strength. If a sample is large enough, a difference of any magnitude may be significant. Because Stouffer's study was based on a large sample, over-all differences as small as 3 or 5 per cent are statistically meaningful; however, comparisons involving small subgroups (resulting from multi-variate cross-tabulation) require differences of 10 to 15 per cent before generalizations can be reliably justified.

This inevitable sampling error is augmented by the possibility of bias attributable to ambiguous wording of questions, deliberate or unconscious distortion by respondents, partiality of interviewers, slovenly editing and transcribing, or incorrect or improper statistical computation. Stouffer tried to minimize such errors by pretesting the schedule of questions, directing interviewers to be alert for respondents' deceptions and their own tendency to lead, setting up quality control checks, and employing trained and experienced interviewers, code clerks, and statistical assistants. Although it would be foolish to believe that bias was eliminated, it probably was not so great as to invalidate generalizations.

Interpretation of Results

These interviews of 6,466 people led Stouffer to the following conclusions:[12]

> Without exception, each of the 14 types of community leaders tends to be more willing to respect the civil rights of socialists, atheists, those suspected of disloyalty who deny they are Communists, and self-avowed Communists than either the rank and file in the same cities as the leaders or the national cross-section.
> Very few Americans are worried or even deeply concerned about . . . the internal Communist threat . . . or are really worried about the threat to civil liberties.
> The data showed that the older generation was less

tolerant of nonconformists than the younger genera-
tion; also, that within each group the less educated
were less tolerant than the better educated.

Women tend, with small but consistent difference,
to be less tolerant than men with respect to nonconformists like socialists, atheists, or Communists, or
suspected nonconformists.

When asked what Communists believe in, the national cross-section most frequently mentioned "anti-
religion," while "government ownership of property"
was also high on the list.

There is something about people with more schooling which equips them to make discriminations, to appreciate the principles of civil rights, and to handle a
value conflict in a more tolerant way than others.

There is a consistent relationship, within our samples
as a whole and within each of a variety of sub-groups,
between perception of the internal Communist danger
and tolerance. Those who see the danger as greatest
tend to be the most intolerant.

These attitudes have interesting and important implications for the future of the nation. To select the
first conclusion as an example, the fact that community
leaders are more likely than the rank and file to extend
civil rights to nonconformists implies strong support
for civic leadership toward teaching historic American
respect for divergent opinions. The final statement sug-
gests that a decrease in the felt internal Communist
threat might be accompanied by increased American
tolerance of nonconformity, or that an increase in the
threat—or belief in its increase—might result in rising
intolerance.

Action and Policy

What do the answers to Stouffer's initial questions
mean for people influential enough to do something
about them? Clearly, there is no evidence that the
citizenry is "suffering from quivering fear or from an
anxiety neurosis about the internal Communist threat.

If there is a sickness, the clinical symptoms are more like dietary deficiency."[13]

Three major classes of people have responsibilities toward preservation of individual liberties in the United States: directors of the mass media of communication (the press, radio, and television), national political leaders (members of Congress, State and Defense Departments, and other agencies), and local community leaders (elected officials, leading businessmen, ministers, lawyers, and interest groups). For most people, newspapers, radio, and television provide the main source—and for many the only source—of information about threats to civil liberties. The responsibility of these media is tremendous because readers, listeners, and viewers place so much trust in their reports. National political leaders have an obligation not to exploit the Communist threat or flee controversy for fear that they will not be re-elected or re-appointed. Yet this survey showed that only a minority of the populace claimed to know the opinions of even the most prominent national figures concerning Communists and how to handle them. Local leaders probably have greater impact on education than upon action. It is at the grass roots level that children learn to understand and apply the Bill of Rights.

Thus we observe in this chapter an example of the application of sociological research to a subject so emotional as to imply maximum imperviousness to scientific investigation. The topic itself is highly controversial, and the principal investigator and probably all of his assistants held powerful opinions on the subject. Yet information was secured, results reported and evaluated, and inferences partially trusted—all under the aegis of fallible science.

VIII

What Sociology Is

*

After seven chapters identifying basic concepts, explaining how sociologists acquire and analyze data, and illustrating these research operations, the question with which the book began—what is this thing called sociology?—should be answerable. The entire book has been a reply.

It may seem curiously inappropriate that a book attempting to describe contemporary sociology is devoted primarily to research methods and only secondarily to results. However, in defining an intellectual subject, research procedures may be quite as important as substantive findings. Otherwise we may be compelled to accept the popular definition of sociologists which includes John O'Hara, Pearl Buck, and Edward Albee. After all, novelists often draw social conclusions, and playwrights as well as sociologists discourse about people. Physicians are distinguished as a group as much by the set of techniques they use as by the subjects with which they are concerned; so too are automobile mechanics, carpenters, and tree surgeons. Yet all five of these types of specialists do work that is also performed by laymen—observing class differentials, healing cuts, grinding valves, building cabinets, and pruning oak trees. What identifies the professional is his greater ability to make skillful use of the tools of his trade: the sample survey, the stethoscope, the torque wrench, the electric drill, and the saw. In fact, most of the specialist's time is spent in the operation of one or another of his tools. In intellectual or academic disciplines these tools are largely concepts and procedures rather than physical implements; such is the case in sociology.

Modern sociology has been defined as "the scientific study of the phenomena arising out of the group relations of human beings."[1] The phrasing "scientific study of the phenomena" is adopted deliberately to signalize that sociology is neither an action program nor one of the humanistic subjects. Actionists and philosophers are often fond of sociology and sometimes even claim that their proposals or writings stem from sociological thought (which occasionally is true), but contemporary sociology is distinguished from actionism by its noninterventionist orientation and separated from the humanistic disciplines by its insistence on empiricism. Let us look briefly at these quasi-sociologies.

Not An Attempt To Change

Sociology has nothing to do with socialism, despite the misleading and hence unfortunate nomenclatural resemblance. Scientific sociology is neither a radical nor even a reform movement.

Reform, however, is often a motive for studying sociology, and many people, including some sociologists, are fond of applying sociological knowledge (and, more frequently, speculation) toward alleviating human distress—for example, clearing slums, improving race relations, lowering the divorce rate, or curbing juvenile delinquency. Yet such projects, notwithstanding their consonance with the origins of sociology, are not elements of modern sociology. They are marginal to the field in somewhat the same way that social work is marginal.

Social work is allied to sociology by virtue of its use of sociological and related findings to facilitate adjustment of individual or family relations with other persons and groups. Social workers try to remove maladjustments without altering the basic framework of society—a task which sociologists respect but which they do not perform professionally. Not only does social work call for different skills and an ameliorative rather than a fact-finding orientation, but social workers also earn a different academic degree—the M.S.W. (Master of Social Work) rather than the M.A. or M.S.

Social engineering is still farther from sociology, dealing as it does with the creation and establishment of new institutional structures in the culture. Social engineers, copying other engineers, start with a problem and apply sociological principles and laws to solving that problem. Hence the apparent similarity to sociology. Examples showing differences, however, are numerous: thus while sociologists seek factual information about family relationships, social engineers try to remodel family organization; whereas sociologists make unbiased studies to learn how leaders arise in social groups, social engineers attempt to manipulate the group toward a certain leadership structure.

Sociologists *qua* sociologists differ from socialists, reformers, social workers, and social engineers for one dominant reason. They seek knowledge; the other four types seek change—sometimes minor changes within the existing social order, sometimes major alterations of the social system, but always some form of change. Motives vary also, from curiosity among sociologists to correction of social ills among the nonsociologists. This is not to say that sociologists are better, but merely that they differ in purpose, procedures, and results.

Lest this ideal depiction of sociologists give the oversimplified impression that they all spend their entire working or waking hours unbiasedly collecting factual evidence, five qualifications need to be made. First, some people are only part-time sociologists; they may also be part-time social workers, for instance. Second, others posing as sociologists are not in fact accredited —because not properly trained. Third, this book portrays what we may call "the new breed" of sociologists; older sociologists often conform to different professional molds. Fourth, some sociologists—new as well as old—frequently do not achieve objectivity, and even the best social scientists probably have failed upon one occasion or another. Finally, all sociologists hold other statuses and play other roles in addition to their professional ones, and in many of these capacities they deviate from their occupational habits (for example, as fathers they may try to improve their children's school, as citizens they may want to stamp out crime, or as taxpayers they may hold highly charged views on government spending). In sum, these pages delineate competent modern sociologists acting as sociologists; but for several reasons at various times they do deviate from the role of scientific sociologist.

Not One of the Humanities

Just as sociology is not essentially humanitarian, so also it is not a part of the humanities, as are history, literature, art, and philosophy. Social historians such as Harry Elmer Barnes, social novelists on the order of John P. Marquand, socially conscious artists such as José Orozco, and social philosophers like John Dewey may make important quasi-sociological contributions. Sociologists, however, are a different breed.

Consider a legal analogy. In 1933, Morris R. Cohen, the distinguished philosopher, compared three different approaches to the law. Legal history, he wrote, describes what the courts have decided at a given place and time. Normative jurisprudence asks what men ought to do to attain certain ends. Legal sociology involves finding abstract uniformities or recurring patterns that make one case like another.[2] Consonantly, descriptive history asks what men did; normative morality tells us what they should have done in the past or ought to do in the future; and sociology forms descriptive generalizations concerning what they actually do under given conditions.

Notice the distinguishing attribute: sociology investigates interrelationships between two or more variables for the purpose of discovering consistent regularities or laws of social behavior, History, literature, art, and philosophy are all charged in part with a responsibility to disclose human aspirations and fallibilities, but they do not do so in a scientific fashion, framing testable hypotheses, comparing them with observed data, and, if successful, formulating generalities or laws. Thus the humanities do not explain specifically and systematically why behavior takes the forms it does—or what makes men tick—although they may provide significant insights and suggest hypotheses for such scientific study.

A Behavioral Science

The term "behavioral sciences" has come into prominence since about 1950 to characterize those academic disciplines that seek to establish laws describing and explaining human thoughts and actions. Behavioral scientists gather empirical evidence in objective ways, subject to questioning by others through replication and testing. Their primary intent is to understand human behavior in much the same sense as that in which physical scientists understand their subjects. Their ultimate purpose (dare we say, hope?) is to learn how to predict human actions, in a similar manner to that of physical scientists in their fields.

The category "behavioral science" includes sociology, psychology, and part of anthropology; occasionally

it is taken to embrace economics and government
(though their inclusion has been challenged); and it
omits geography, history, philosophy, and law—all of
which have at one time or another been grouped with
the foregoing subjects under the traditional rubric of
social science. The distinction between social science
and behavioral science turns about two foci: objectives
and methods. Both types of discipline study people,
but behavioral science aims at discovery of empirical
regularities. Consequently, although both use reason
and logic, behavioral science differs by actually being
scientific (the term "social science" is a misnomer).
To summarize, the humanities and certain social sciences study phenomena each of which they regard as
unique, whereas the behavioral sciences study phenomena which they regard as recurrent—though frequently the two types of scholars are in fact inspecting
precisely the same events and situations. It may be
noted further that "The Study of the Unique" is a recurrent subtitle for anti-behavioral science speeches
and articles, which fact in itself might be a lesson.

In respect to objectives and research methods, sociology bears greater kinship to psychology than to any
other academic discipline (with the possible exception
of anthropology). Note, however, that this kinship ex-
tends not to clinical psychology, which is cousin to
social work, but to experimental psychology, which
attempts to understand human behavior by using many
of the same methodological procedures as modern
sociology: hypotheses, matched control groups, samples, statistical measures, and qualified conclusions.
Experimental psychology thus shares most of the ideas
presented in Chapters II through VI, though differing
from sociology in that whereas psychologists work
largely on the individual, sociologists take as their
specialty the examination of interindividual relations.
The two fields do meet frequently, however, as is evidenced by examples provided in earlier chapters; for
instance, among the principal authors of the four vol-

umes of *The American Soldier* are several representatives of each discipline.

An Art or a Science?

Sociology also shares with psychology the chronic question: is it an art or a science? Most sociologists have long since tired of this issue, but it is one that must be faced—the customer may not always be right, but you had best answer his query.

This question is founded on several misconceptions about science. Generally the questioner seems to have in mind a more fundamental question that he is too polite to ask: is it even possible for sociology to be scientific? Newspaper columns frequently state the first or manifest question and then proceed to answer the second or latent one by reminding readers what they think they already know: that is, that man cannot study himself or his attitudes unbiasedly, that sociological experts do not agree, that certainty is not obtained in sociology, and that social policy decisions are always debatable. To respond: men can study themselves and their attitudes objectively; the fact that expert opinions differ in sociology no more removes the subject from the category of science than does similar disagreement—and there is much of it—in physics; absolute certainty is inherently unattainable in science; and policy decisions are not a part of sociology itself but fall rather in the bailiwicks of philosophy, law, and politics.

Disclaimers aside, the question still remains: is sociology an art or a science? Answer: it is both—sometimes one, sometimes the other. Modern sociologists are generally men of science, and the field seems committed to increasing emphasis on scientific research. Alongside this core of gatherers of hard facts, however, are ranged nonscientific scholars studying the same subjects but without the scientific paraphernalia. Some contemporary sociologists regard these fellow-travelers as remnants of a dying humanistic tradition, but it seems a shame to waste brainpower of these nonscientific contributors simply because they refuse to adopt certain research techniques. Hence the armchair sociologists will probably continue to form a part of the field for many years to come, contributing colorful and even brilliant insights from their sometimes fruitful imaginations. To be sure, these intriguing insights are not exclusively the province of old-style sociologists—as witnessed by the many scientific sociologists endowed with equally vivid and germinal ideas—but it is the latter's general practice to avoid publishing such speculations until buttressed by systematic research.

Imagination is thus seen to be an essential part of sociological thought, whether scientific or nonscientific. Albert Einstein's emphasis on the imaginative leap is supplemented by the serendipity principle enunciated by Robert K. Merton: that is, if the research investigator is alert to serendipitous or unanticipated clues and avoids the dangers of premature specifications and overeager drawing of conclusions, his flexibility may pay off through recognition of the value of anomalous findings.[3] A researcher who is prepared to perceive, accept, and manipulate intellectually the unsought and unexpected results of sociological inquiry is in a position to extend or adapt existing theory or formulate original hypotheses. From Louis Pasteur's axiom that chance favors the prepared mind, the inference is clearly drawn that the informed scholar who preserves an attitude of skeptical doubt is able to revise his theorizing to incorporate unpremeditated information. And so it seems that imaginative insight can be turned to scientific ends—in fact, without imagination, scientific tools rust and hard facts wither on the vine. Perhaps the moral of this story is that curiosity is the essential ingredient of sociological knowledge—as, for that matter, of any other knowledge.

Thus upon examination the art-science antithesis

tends to evanesce. Sociology contains elements of both science and cleverly contrived nonscience (which is apparently what is meant by "art").

Deciding To Be a Sociologist

If most people cannot decide whether sociology is an art or a science, and if they are unsure even what sociology is and what sociologists do, it is not surprising that commitment to sociology as a career does not often come before the last year or two of undergraduate work; frequently its choice as an occupation is not made until after the passage of several years of postgraduate employment or a year or two of graduate study. Interviews with 1960-1961 graduate students revealed the following distribution of times of decision to pursue graduate study in sociology: before entering college, none; early in college, 8 per cent; some time in college, 25 per cent; junior or senior year, 20 per cent; after graduation but before entering graduate school, 20 per cent; and after beginning graduate study in another subject, 28 per cent.[4] Thus the decision to study sociology appears usually to involve not an initial career choice, but rather a transfer from another field of study and abandonment of another vocational objective.

One reason for the exceptional lateness of entrance into a course of professional training for sociology is the lack of a public image of the sociologist himself.[5] Young children in our society play at being nurses, policemen, astronauts, storekeepers, and racing drivers, but unfamiliar with sociologists, they cannot pretend to be one. Later, after they have heard of sociology, they still rarely elect it as an occupation, even tentatively. To most adolescents, there is little about sociology that stimulates their imagination or ambition; unlike chemistry, medicine, acting, or writing, sociology has no magic to perform. Moreover, sociological ideas generally appear at first encounter to be obscure, absurd, obvious, unimportant, or laughable; for most persons, only in adulthood comes recognition of the significance and fascination of sociological reasoning and events.

Absence of sociology courses in elementary and secondary schools means that first academic exposure to the subject usually comes, if at all, in college. And then the selection of sociology as a "major" is often not based on criteria that augur well for a commitment to scientific sociology. The curiosity about social problems and zeal for alleviation of social ills which motivate many sociology students, however laudable when put to other uses, are not conducive to hardheaded thinking about social behavior. If they do go on to graduate work, students whose conceptions of the field are unrealistic or at variance with contemporary professional roles and requirements tend to depart from the field, disillusioned or bewildered. Other departures are prompted by inadequacy of undergraduate preparation in the one or two foreign languages customarily required for the M.A. or Ph.D., as well as, more importantly, ignorance of scientific method, logic, and mathematics, some knowledge of which is essential to thorough mastery of modern sociology. Of beginning graduate students in sociology, "a great majority have not had even one course in the calculus, without which one cannot be considered ready for more than superficial study of a 'hard' science involving quantitative methods or formal models"; moreover, "many have taken only the undemanding kind of science courses customarily offered for students not primarily interested in science" and consequently have not learned scientific skills or orientation in any intellectual discipline.[6]

Thus espousal of a scientific orientation toward sociology comes even later and less frequently than does acceptance of the substantive findings of sociology. Moreover, sociological competence needs to be built on a foundation of logical rigor and social maturity—

a combination not ordinarily achieved until one has come of age educationally and in experience of the world.

Becoming a Sociologist

Regardless of how sociology is classified or defined, academic training is necessary to qualify one as a sociologist. This training is confined to the college level and above. A handful of high schools do offer courses in sociology, but they cannot make a sociologist of the student. Professional standing demands at least a B.A. and generally a graduate degree. Membership in the national professional organization—the American Sociological Association—normally presupposes an advanced degree: in 1959, 62 per cent of the members held a doctorate, 27 per cent held another graduate degree, and 11 per cent apparently held no graduate degree.[7] A serious career as a sociologist cannot reasonably be founded upon possession merely of a bachelor's degree. The B.A. in sociology does prove a starting point for employment in market research, elementary and secondary teaching, public relations, and a variety of jobs designated in some such fashion as social science analyst, but this kind of work does not qualify a person as a sociologist. Furthermore, promotion generally requires additional academic training. If one is not to remain in an occupational dead end, he must attain at least an M.A. and preferably a Ph.D. to be able to compete for the more stimulating appointments offering independence of action and higher pay.

Today, the United States Office of Education reports a large number of educational institutions at which sociological training may be secured. In the 1961-1962 academic year, 679 institutions conferred baccalaureate degrees, 135 awarded master's degrees, and 46 granted doctorates. The number of persons receiving these degrees was 8,132 bachelor's, 578 master's, and

173 doctor's. Both the number of institutions and the numbers of degrees granted show a long-run tendency to increase; by 1969-1970 it is estimated that United States colleges will award more than 15,000 bachelor's, 900 master's, and 300 doctor's degrees—nearly doubling the annual production in eight years. Women dominate among baccalaureate recipients, but graduate degree recipients are predominantly men.[8]

Jobs are expected to more than keep pace with this increasing man-power. Colleges will probably need more sociology Ph.D.'s than the country is expected to produce during the rest of the 1960 decade; perforce, many new teaching positions will be filled by persons on the M.A. level. Future demand from government, business, and industry is more difficult to project, but it too is expected to exceed the anticipated supply.[9] Therefore persons entering course work toward a degree in sociology should have no fears concerning their occupational opportunities.

Sociologists at Work

Let us now return for a moment to the opening question, what is sociology? The subject has been defined in this book in terms of the basic concepts sociologists use and the means whereby they acquire and analyze information. The first part of this chapter explains what sociology is not. Now, what is it? Sociology is the way in which sociologists think. It is what sociologists do to add to man's knowledge. But it may also be defined by the professional activities in which sociologists engage.

What is it then that professional sociologists do to justify their salaries? Many things: research, which consists of discovering heretofore unknown facts or substantiating hitherto incompletely supported hypotheses; scholarship, which means becoming expert in and keeping up with the literature of the field; teaching, usually on the college level; and a myriad of administrative, ameliorative, and other applications. The nonscientific character of much of this work also holds of course for physicists, chemists, and workers in other undeniably scientific fields.

Sociologists frequently wear two hats, one designating their major activity and one indicating their part-time or moonlighting work. Thus college professors supplement their income and often gain enriching experience by outside lecturing, writing, consulting, and advising governmental, business, and industrial organizations. Nonacademic sociologists do the same—often teaching a course or two in a nearby college's evening division.

Sources of support are also diversified. Money for research is supplied by Federal and local governments, private foundations, commercial and industrial corporations, and universities. Several Federal agencies, notably the National Science Foundation, the National Institutes of Mental Health, and the Department of Defense, sponsor research done by individual college professors and by nonprofit research organizations. The Ford Foundation and other private foundations provide a few additional millions of dollars. Businesses and industrial firms comprise the largest single source of funds for social science research, but most such "research and development" money is spent on marketing research and other applied interests which contribute very little to the advance of sociological knowledge. Nonetheless, much—perhaps most—of this research funded by nonacademic organizations is performed on college campuses by faculty in chunks of time free from their teaching duties. Colleges and universities themselves provide further support out of their own resources. The sum of all this effort is an expenditure of many million dollars annually on basic research, plus a somewhat greater amount for applied research.

Although other nations also contribute money and manpower to promote sociological research as well as to teach courses in sociology, the United States is indisputably the foremost country in advancing and disseminating sociological knowledge. This contemporary domination of world sociology by the United States represents a change from sociology's first flourishing in nineteenth-century France, England, and Germany. The first American academic department of sociology was not established until 1893 at the University of Chicago, and the American Sociological Association was formed by a hundred-odd scholars in 1905. Today, however, the field has grown so phenomenally that nearly all colleges have sociology departments and the number of sociologists approaches 10,000. This pre-eminence of the United States in teaching and research has been accompanied by a corresponding supremacy in the quality and quantity of jobs available to sociologists.

Academic Employment

The most common occupational outlet for sociologists is college teaching, frequently accompanied by research and presumably always including scholarly study in one's specialty. A survey of the 6,345 members of the American Sociological Association in 1959 evinced the following occupational affiliations: liberal arts colleges, 59 per cent; professional schools, 11 per cent; Federal government, 5 per cent; business and industry, 6 per cent; local health and welfare agencies, 6 per cent; miscellaneous and retired, 9 per cent; and no information, 4 per cent.[10] Note that 70 per cent of the members are principally employed in teaching or research on the college or university level. There appears to be a pronounced trend toward affiliation with graduate and professional schools, accompanied by a corresponding decline (relatively, not in absolute numbers) in undergraduate teaching.

Academic appointments fall into two broad categories: teaching and research, with the large majority of openings being of the former type. Colleges and universities hire sociologists to teach classes not only in sociology departments, but also in schools of social work, law, medicine, education, and business. The Ph.D. is normally required for permanency. A few high schools now offer a few courses in sociology, but sociological competence is not prerequisite and therefore this is not considered an occupational outlet for professional sociologists.

University research organizations utilizing sociology are currently expanding in number and size. Many universities have permanent social research bureaus or laboratories, some employing dozens of sociologists to do research design, interviewing, calculating, and writing of results. Such jobs generally call for a Ph.D. on the supervisory level, the M.A. on the journeyman level, and the B.A. on the apprentice or clerical level.

Government Jobs

Federal, state, and local governments hire sociologists in considerable numbers. Federal agencies welcoming sociologists include especially the Bureau of the Census, the Children's Bureau, the National Institutes of Health, and various other arms of the Department of Health, Education, and Welfare. Ever since World War II the Army, Navy, and Air Force have hired sociologists to perform attitude and opinion research, and there is even a specialty called military sociology.

State, county, and city employers include city planning commissions, parole boards, housing authorities, penal organizations, welfare agencies, and many others whose primary functions are not sociological but who have incidental need of one or several employees boasting sociological training. Public health and medical sociology, like military sociology a young field, is itself coming to offer a considerable number of opportunities to specialists in small groups, formal organizations, communications, and opinion change. Mental health is a budding field for sociologists with some training in psychology.

Private welfare agencies, hospitals, counseling centers, youth groups, churches, clinics, settlement houses, and nursery schools also need and hire sociologists. These eleemosynary and quasi-public "helping" agencies often prefer social workers, but they do accept sociologists for many positions.

Business and Industry

Commercial and manufacturing organizations are turning increasingly to sociology departments for staffing. Polling and market research groups need people skilled in both statistics and in one of the social sciences. Real estate expertise requires knowledge of social ecological principles. Advertising agencies drain off promising graduate students to account executive positions with the lure of high incomes and promotions. Insurance companies hire demographers and social statisticians. Public relations too impinges on sociology. Elsewhere, sociologists are invading factories to ascertain influences on production rates, reactions to work conditions, and causes of absenteeism. Sales promotion directors ask sociologists to help "out-psych" prospective purchasers.

Since sociology is a new field in comparison with the physical sciences and even with other social sciences, many organizations have been slow to recognize the value of employing sociologists. But today sociologists are becoming as well accepted by personnel officers as the psychologists and economists they have been hiring for several decades. In the future, increasing numbers of sociologists will probably be working in government agencies, business concerns and industrial plants. This trend should result in decreasing proportions (though not decreasing numbers) of sociologists employed in academic institutions as their occupational activities become more diversified.

Fields of Specialization

In addition to examining the places of employment, further clarification of the roles and functions of sociologists stems from consideration of their major areas of competence. In 1959, the dozen leading fields of specialization reported by members of the American Sociological Association were, beginning with the most frequently reported: social psychology, research methodology, marriage and the family, organizations, theory, population, race and ethnic relations, criminology, cultural anthropology, community relations, public opinion and communication, and industrial sociology. Fields exhibiting the greatest increases in number of affiliates over the 1950-1959 period were: (a) medical sociology, mental health, and aging; (b) stratification, occupations, organizations, and small groups; and (c) sociology of law, religion, art, music, and literature. These trends evidently reflect in part a growing emphasis on practice and application.[11]

Another guide to what sociology is all about lies in the topics covered in introductory textbooks, presumably a locus in which the authors try to sum up the current state of sociological knowledge in meaningful categories. Among twenty-four basic texts published from 1952 through 1959 (of which no one book captured more than one-sixth of the total sales) a dozen themes were dealt with extensively (defined by inclusion in the table of contents or substantial inclusion in the index) by at least twenty books: culture, scientific methods, personality, groups, the family, social change, religion, race, population, class and caste, economic institutions, and education.[12] Clearly, not all of the twenty-four books agreed on how to compartmentalize sociology, but it can be stated fairly that there was considerable acceptance of these twelve topics. Allowing for differences between student-oriented and professional terminology, this list appars generally consistent with that obtained from sociology association members describing their own specialties.

A second version of the interpretation that "sociology is what sociologists teach"[13] led to a study in 1957 of the catalogs of 607 American colleges. Following the ubiquitous introductory sociology and general anthropology courses, the study found that the most commonly offered courses were, in order, marriage and the family, criminology, social problems, social work, deviance, social psychology, theory, and race and ethnic groups.[14] But though somewhat the same topics appeared as in the two previous listings, discrepancies do exist. Their presence is primarily attributable to the duality of functions of undergraduate teaching: service and professional preparation. Service courses teach facts and accepted interpretations to students seeking a baccalaureate in majors other than sociology and also to sociology majors having a nonprofessional orientation; pre-professional courses teach core material to students intending to follow sociology careers. The two approaches are not incompatible, yet textbooks and instructors find it difficult to satisfy both aims truly well at the same time in a single course.

Certain fields are so important that familiarity with them is widely accepted as an essential condition for sociological competence; consequently formal course instruction on the professional level always contains and usually requires these subjects. Two such areas—social theory and research methods—are almost universally required in Ph.D. and M.A. examinations; sometimes they are singled out as the sole elements of the first battery of graduate examinations, to be followed later by testing on two or three topics selected by the student from among a set of areas permitted by the department. Theory and methods are often referred to as the "core" of sociological training: if a student cannot demonstrate that he understands these two fields, he fails in his quest for the degree; if he exhibits adequate knowledge of them, he may qualify for the final stage of degree preparation—the writing of a thesis.

Conclusion

From the foregoing pages it is evident that the study of people in groups is reaching maturity not only as an intellectual discipline adding to man's knowledge but also, as its practitioners apply this knowledge, as a means of making modern life more manageable and meaningful to the individual and more efficient and manipulable for the organization. Befitting a discipline aspiring to the sobriquet "science," sociology's accomplishments impress laymen as sometimes laudable, sometimes distressing, and sometimes just plain incomprehensible.

All in all, however, sociology is becoming not only scientific but also financially rewarding to its researchers, teachers, and practitioners, especially those with methodological and statistical training. The new sociologists seem to be succeeding both on the basis of soundness of scholarly research and also in the practical matter of income-producing jobs. The sociological mills are grinding rapidly and well enough to justify Merton's paraphrase of Galileo, that sociology is "a very new science of a very ancient subject."[15]

Notes

*

Chapter I.

1 Cole Porter, "What Is This Thing Called Love?", *Wake Up and Dream*, New York, 1929; and Wolfgang Amadeus Mozart, "Voi, che sapete, che cosa e amor?", *The Marriage of Figaro*, K. 492, Vienna, 1786, Act II.

2 Émile Durkheim, *Le suicide*, Paris, F. Alcan, 1897 (translated by John A. Spaulding and George Simpson and published as *Suicide*, Glencoe, Ill., Free Press, 1951).

3 Robin M. Williams Jr., *American Society*, New York, Alfred A. Knopf, 1960, pp. 415-468.

4 R. J. Havighurst and Hilda Taba, *Adolescent Character and Personality*, New York, John Wiley and Sons, 1949.

5 Albert K. Cohen, *Delinquent Boys: The Subculture of the Gang*, Glencoe, Ill., Free Press, 1959.

6 William Graham Sumner, *Folkways*, Boston, Ginn and Co., 1906, Chap. 15.

7 Eric Larrabee, *The Self-Conscious Society*, New York, Doubleday and Co., 1960.

8 Jane Richardson and A. L. Kroeber, "Three Centuries of Women's Dress Fashions: A Quantitative Analysis," *Anthropological Records*, Vol. V, No. 2, October 1940, pp. 111-153.

9 Ralph Linton, *The Study of Man*, New York, Appleton-Century Co., 1936, p. 115.

10 Kingsley Davis, *Human Society*, New York, The Macmillan Co., 1949, p. 208.

11 Wolfgang Kohler, *The Mentality of Apes*, New York, Humanities Press, 1925, p. 293.

12 George Herbert Mead, *Mind, Self and Society*, Chicago, University of Chicago Press, 1934, p. 154.

13 Sumner, *Folkways*.

14 Charles Horton Cooley, *Social Organizations*, New York, Charles Scribner's Sons, 1909, p. 23.

15 Herbert H. Hyman, *The Psychology of Status*, Archives of Psychology, No. 269, 1942.

16 Samuel A. Stouffer *et al.*, *The American Soldier: Adjustment during Army Life*, Vol. I of *Studies in Social Psychology in World War II*, Princeton, Princeton University Press, 1949, p. 256.

17 Robert H. Lowie, *Primitive Society*, New York, Boni and Liveright, 1920, p. 67.

18 W. Lloyd Warner and Paul S. Lunt, *Social Life of a Modern Community*, New Haven, Yale University Press, 1941.

19 Allison Davis, Burleigh B. Gardner, and Mary R. Gardner, *Deep South*, Chicago, University of Chicago Press, 1941, Chap. III.

20 Kingsley Davis, "The Myth of Functional Analysis as a Special Method in Sociology and Anthropology," *American Sociological Review*, Vol. XXIV, No. 6, December 1956, p. 757.

21 Bronislaw Malinowski, "Anthropology," *Encyclopedia Britannica*, thirteenth edition, Supplementary Volume I, 1926, p. 132.

22 A. R. Radcliffe-Brown, "On the Concept of Function in Social Science," *American Anthropologist*, Vol. XXXVII, 1935, p. 397.

23 Robert K. Merton, *Social Theory and Social Structure*, Glencoe, Ill., Free Press, 1949, p. 50.

24 Kingsley Davis, "The Sociology of Prostitution," *American Sociological Review*, Vol. II, No. 5, October 1937, pp. 744-755.

25 Merton, *Social Theory*, p. 51.

26 Thorstein Veblen, *The Theory of the Leisure Class*, New York, The Macmillan Co., 1899, Part IV.

27 Merton, *Social Theory*, pp. 70 and 372.

28 Harold F. Gosnell, *Machine Politics: Chicago Model*, Chicago, University of Chicago Press, 1937.

29 Lincoln Steffens, *Autobiography*, Chatauqua, N. Y., Chatauqua Press, 1931, p. 618.

30 Merton, *Social Theory*, p. 79.

31 Grayson Kirk, "Responsibilities of the Educated Man," *Graduate Faculties Newsletter*, Columbia University, May 1964, p. 2.

32 Charles Percy Snow, *The Two Cultures: and a Second Look*, London, Cambridge University Press, 1963, p. 67. Also

cf. essays by Robert Bierstedt and Charles H. Page in Page (ed.), *Sociology and Contemporary Education,* New York, Random House, 1964.

Chapter II.

[1] Robert K. Merton, *Social Theory and Social Structure,* Glencoe, Ill., Free Press, 1949, p. 83.

[2] William Graham Sumner, *Folkways,* Boston, Ginn and Co., 1906, p. 13.

[3] Robert Bierstedt, "The Limitations of Anthropological Methods in Sociology," *American Journal of Sociology,* Vol. LIV, No. 1, July 1948, pp. 27-28.

[4] Sumner, *Folkways,* p. 14.

[5] Robert H. Lowie, *Are We Civilized?* New York, Harcourt, Brace and Co., 1929, p. 4.

[6] Rudyard Kipling, "In the Neolithic Age," 1895.

[7] Weston LaBarre, "The Cultural Basis of Emotions and Gestures," *Journal of Personality,* Vol. XVI, No. 1, September 1947, pp. 49-68.

[8] Kingsley Davis, *Human Society,* New York, The Macmillan Co., 1949, p. 13.

[9] John Morley, *A Biographical Critique of Voltaire,* in Francois Marie Arouet de Voltaire, *Works,* Paris, E. R. DuMont, 1901, Vol. XLII, p. 19.

[10] Merton, *Social Theory,* p. 304.

[11] Davis, *Human Society,* pp. 10-11.

[12] Alfred C. Kinsey, Wardell B. Pomeroy, and Clyde E. Martin, *Sexual Behavior in the Human Male,* Philadelphia, W. B. Saunders Co., 1948, pp. 11-12.

[13] Louis Wirth, "Responsibility of Social Science," in Harold M. Dorr (ed.), "Social Implications of Modern Science," *The Annals of the American Academy of Political and Social Science,* Vol. CCXLIX, January 1947.

[14] Georges Cuvier; quoted in Claude Bernard, *An Introduction to the Study of Experimental Medicine,* New York, Dover Publications, 1957, p. 60 (originally published in Paris in 1865).

[15] *Ibid.,* pp. 59-60.

[16] Fritz Machlup, "Are the Social Sciences Really Inferior?" *The Southern Economic Journal,* Vol. XXVII, No. 3, January 1961, pp. 173-184.

[17] Ernest Nagel, *Logic Without Metaphysics,* Glencoe, Ill., Free Press, 1956, p. 254.

[18] *Webster's New International Dictionary of the English Language,* Springfield, Mass., G. and C. Merriam Co., Second Edition, Unabridged, 1934, 1956.

[19] Mildred Parten, in Henry Pratt Fairchild (ed.), *Dictionary of Sociology,* Ames, Iowa, Littlefield, Adams and Co., 1944, p. 332.

20 Ernest Greenwood, *Experimental Sociology*, New York, King's Crown Press, 1945.

21 Richard B. Braithwaite, *Scientific Explanation*, London, Cambridge University Press, 1953.

22 John M. Somerville, "Umbrellaology; or, Methodology in Social Science," *Philosophy of Science*, Vol. VIII, October 1941, pp. 557-566.

23 Albert Einstein, *The World As I See It* (translated by Alan Harris), New York, Covici Friede, 1934, p. 91.

24 Nagel, *Logic Without Metaphysics*, p. 255.

25 Bernard, *Experimental Medicine*, pp. 32-34.

26 Robert M. MacIver, *Social Causation*, Boston, Ginn and Co., 1942.

27 Francis R. Allen, Hornell Hart, Delbert C. Miller, William F. Ogburn, and Meyer F. Nimkoff, *Technology and Social Change*, New York, Appleton-Century-Crofts Inc., 1957, p. 77.

Chapter III.

1 Robert S. Lynd and Helen M. Lynd, *Middletown*, New York, Harcourt Brace and Co., 1929.

2 E. Franklin Frazier, *The Negro Family in the United States*, Chicago, University of Chicago Press, 1939.

3 Karl Pearson, "On the Change in Expectation of Life in Man During a Period of circa 2000 Years," *Biometrika*, Vol. I, 1901-1902, p. 261; and John D. Durand, "Mortality Estimates from Roman Tombstone Inscriptions," *American Journal of Sociology*, Vol. LXV, No. 4, January 1960, pp. 365-373.

4 H. D. F. Kitto, *The Greeks*, Penguin Books, London, 1951; and Charles Seltman, *Women in Antiquity*, New York, Collier Books, 1962.

5 Sigmund Freud, *Leonardo da Vinci: A Study in Psycho-Sexuality*, New York, Random House, 1947.

6 William F. Whyte, *Street Corner Society*, Chicago, University of Chicago Press, 1943.

7 Howard S. Becker, "The Professional Dance Musician and His Audience," *American Journal of Sociology*, Vol. LVII, No. 2, September 1951, pp. 136-144; and William Bruce Cameron, "Sociological Notes on the Jam Session," *Social Forces*, Vol. XXXIII, No. 2, December 1954, pp. 177-182.

8 F. J. Roethlisberger and W. J. Dickson, *Management and the Worker*, Cambridge, Mass., Harvard University Press, 1939.

9 Muzafer Sherif, *The Psychology of Social Norms*, New York, Harper and Brothers, 1936.

10 Solomon E. Asch, *Social Psychology*, Prentice-Hall, New York, 1952, pp. 450-501; and B. P. Cohen, "A Probability Model for Conformity," *Sociometry*, Vol. XXI, No. 1, March 1958, pp. 69-81.

[11] Jerzy Neyman, *Lectures and Conferences on Mathematical Statistics*, Washington, D. C., United States Department of Agriculture, 1938, p. 90.

[12] L. H. C. Tippett, "Random Sampling Numbers," in Karl Pearson, *Tracts for Computers*, No. XV, London, Cambridge University Press, 1927.

[13] M. G. Kendall and B. Babington Smith, "Tables of Random Sampling Numbers," in Karl Pearson, *Tracts for Computers*, No. XXIV, London, Cambridge University Press, 1939.

[14] Rand Corporation, *A Million Random Digits with 100,-000 Normal Deviates*, Glencoe, Ill., Free Press, 1955.

[15] U. S. Bureau of the Census, "The Current Population Survey: A Report on Methodology," Washington, D. C., U. S. Government Printing Office, 1963.

Chapter IV.

[1] Harold F. Gosnell, *Getting Out the Vote*, Chicago, University of Chicago Press, 1927.

[2] Carl I. Hovland, Arthur A. Lumsdaine, and Fred D. Sheffield, *Experiments on Mass Communication*, Vol. III of Samuel A. Stouffer *et al.*, *Studies in Social Psychology in World War II*, Princeton, Princeton University Press, 4 vols., 1949-1950.

[3] Kingsley Davis, "Extreme Social Isolation of a Child," *American Journal of Sociology*, Vol. XLV, No. 4, January 1940, pp. 554-564; and "Final Note on a Case of Extreme Isolation," *American Journal of Sociology*, Vol. LII, No. 5, March 1947, pp. 432-437.

[4] Samuel A. Stouffer, "Some Observations on Study Design," *American Journal of Sociology*, Vol. LV, No. 4, January 1950, pp. 355-361.

[5] Ronald A. Fisher, *The Design of Experiments*, Edinburgh, Oliver and Boyd, 1937, p. 21.

[6] Solomon E. Asch, "Studies in the Principles of Judgments and Attitudes: Determination of Judgments by Group and Ego Standards," *Journal of Social Psychology*, Vol. XII, No. 2, November 1940, pp. 433-465.

[7] John Stuart Mill, *A System of Logic*, London, 1843; and Charles Hartshorne and Paul Weiss (eds.), *Collected Papers of Charles S. Peirce*, Cambridge, Mass., Harvard University Press, 1931.

[8] Mildred B. Parten, *Surveys, Polls, and Samples*, New York, Harper & Brothers, 1950, p. 290.

[9] Jacob L. Moreno, *Who Shall Survive?*, Washington, D. C., Nervous and Mental Disease Publishing Co., 1934.

[10] George A. Lundberg and Margaret Lawsing, "The Sociography of Some Community Relations," *American Sociological Review*, Vol. II, No. 3, June 1937, pp. 318-335.

11 Paul F. Lazarsfeld, "A Conceptual Introduction to Latent Structure Analysis," in Lazarsfeld (ed.), *Mathematical Thinking in the Social Sciences*, Glencoe, Ill., Free Press, 1954, pp. 349-387.

12 Joseph T. Klapper and Charles Y. Glock, "Trial by Newspaper," *Scientific American*, Vol. CLXXX, No. 2, February 1949, pp. 16-21.

13 Claude S. Brinegar, "Mark Twain and the Quintus Curtius Snodgrass Letters: A Statistical Test of Authorship," *Journal of the American Statistical Association*, Vol. LVIII, No. 301, March 1963, pp. 85-96.

14 Bernard Berelson and Patricia J. Salter, "Majority and Minority Americans: An Analysis of Magazine Fiction," *Public Opinion Quarterly*, Vol. X, No. 2, Summer 1946, pp. 168-190.

15 Lyle W. Shannon, "The Opinions of Little Orphan Annie and Her Friends," *Public Opinion Quarterly*, Vol. XVIII, No. 2, Summer 1954, pp. 169-179.

16 L. L. Thurstone and E. J. Chave, *The Measurement of Attitude*, Chicago, University of Chicago Press, 1929.

17 Rensis Likert, "A Technique for the Measurement of Attitudes," *Archives of Psychology*, No. 140, 1932.

18 Louis Guttman, Chaps. 10 and 11 of Samuel A. Stouffer *et al.*, *Measurement and Prediction*, Vol. IV of Stouffer, *Studies in Social Psychology in World War II*, Princeton, Princeton University Press, 4 vols., 1949-1950.

19 S. S. Stevens, "On the Theory of Scales and Measurement," *Science*, Vol. CIII, No. 2684, June 7, 1946, pp. 677-680.

20 James Thurber, "And A Happy New Year," *The New Yorker*, Vol. XXX, No. 47, January 8, 1955, p. 24.

21 Hans Zeisel, *Say It with Figures*, New York, Harper & Brothers, 1950, p. 165.

22 M. J. Moroney, *Facts from Figures*, London, Penguin Books, 1951, p. 321.

Chapter V.

1 U. S. Department of Agriculture, *Climate and Man*, Washington, D. C., U. S. Government Printing Office, 1941, pp. 875 and 1192.

2 Samuel A. Stouffer *et al.*, *The American Soldier: Combat and Its Aftermath*, Vol. II of *Studies in Social Psychology in World War II*, Princeton, Princeton University Press, 1949.

3 Mordecai Ezekiel, *Methods of Correlation Analysis*, New York, John Wiley and Sons, 1941, p. 103.

4 Hugh H. Wolfenden, *The Fundamental Principles of Mathematical Statistics*, Toronto, The Macmillan Co., 1942, p. 320.

5 George W. Snedecor, "Design of Sampling Experiments in the Social Sciences," *Journal of Farm Economics*, Vol. XXI, 1939, pp. 846-855.

6 Alexander McFarlane Mood, *Introduction to the Theory of Statistics*, New York, McGraw-Hill Book Co., 1950, p. 124.

7 Pierre Simon de Laplace, "Essai philosophique sur les probabilités," Introduction to *Théorie analytique des probabilités*, Paris, 1814, p. 152.

8 Frederick Mosteller, Robert E. K. Rourke, and George B. Thomas Jr., *Probability with Statistical Applications*, Reading, Mass., Addison-Wesley Publishing Co., 1961, p. 403.

9 Howard W. Alexander, *Elements of Mathematical Statistics*, New York, John Wiley and Sons, 1961, pp. 16-19; and Samuel Goldberg, *Probability*, Englewood Cliffs, N. J., Prentice-Hall Inc., 1960, pp. 16-20 and 28-36.

10 Paul G. Hoel, *Introduction to Mathematical Statistics*, New York, John Wiley and Sons, 1962, pp. 4-22; and William Feller, *An Introduction to Probability Theory and Its Application*, New York, John Wiley and Sons, Vol. I, 1957, pp. 13-24.

11 Morris H. Hansen, William N. Hurwitz, and William G. Madow, *Sample Survey Methods and Theory*, New York, John Wiley and Sons, 1953, Vol. I, pp. 19-20.

12 Mood, *Theory of Statistics*, p. 136.

13 Richard Doll and A. Bradford Hill, "A Study of the Aetiology of Carcinoma of the Lung," *British Medical Journal*, December 13, 1952, Part 2, pp. 1271-1286.

14 Sidney Siegel, *Nonparametric Statistics*, New York, McGraw-Hill Book Co., 1956, p. 31.

15 John G. Kemeny and J. Laurie Snell, *Finite Markov Chains*, Princeton, D. Van Nostrand Co., 1960.

Chapter VI.

1 W. W. Rouse Ball, *A Short Account of the History of Mathematics*, London, Macmillan and Co., 1908, p. 191.

2 Tobias Dantzig, *Number: The Language of Science*, Garden City, N. Y., Doubleday and Co., 1954, p. 26.

3 Ball, *History of Mathematics*, pp. 192-194.

4 Dantzig, *Number*, p. 16.

5 George Sarton, *A History of Science*, Cambridge, Mass., Harvard University Press, 1952, vol. I, pp. 69-74.

6 Florian Cajori, *A History of the Logarithmic Slide Rule*, New York, Engineering News Publishing Co., 1909.

7 Abraham Wolf, *A History of Science, Technology, and Philosophy in the Sixteenth and Seventeenth Centuries*, London, Allen and Unwin, 1950, pp. 560-563.

8 Abraham Wolf, *A History of Science, Technology, and Philosophy in the Eighteenth Century*, London, Allen and Unwin, 1952, pp. 653-660.

9 Charles Babbage, *Calculating Engines and Selected Writings*, New York, Dover Publications, 1961.

[10] L. F. Menabrea, "Sketch of the Analytical Engine Invented by Charles Babbage," *Bibliotèque Universelle de Genève*, No. 82, October, 1842; translated and extensively annotated by Countess Ada Augusta of Lovelace, in R. Taylor (ed.), *Scientific Memoirs*, London, 1842, Vol. III, pp. 691-731.

[11] Alan M. Turing, "On Computable Numbers, with an Application to the Entscheidungsproblem," *Proceedings of the London Mathematical Society*, Series 2, Vol. XLII, No. 11, November 1936, pp. 230-265.

[12] Herbert George Wells, *Mankind in the Making*, London, Chapman and Hall, 1903.

[13] Bert F. Green Jr., *Digital Computers in Research*, New York, McGraw-Hill Book Co., 1936, p. 4.

[14] Alan M. Turing, "Computing Machinery and Intelligence," *Mind*, Vol. LIX, No. 236, October 1950, pp. 433-460.

[15] Claude E. Shannon and Warren Weaver, *The Mathematical Theory of Communication*, Urbana, University of Illinois Press, 1949.

[16] Franz Adler, "A Unit Concept for Sociology," *American Journal of Sociology*, Vol. LXV, No. 4, January 1960, pp. 356-364. For an anthropologist's analysis of cultural behavior bits, see Marvin Harris, *The Nature of Cultural Things*, New York, Random House, 1964, pp. 26-107.

[17] Morris Zelditch Jr. and William M. Evan, "Simulated Bureaucracies: A Methodological Analysis," in Harold Guetzkow (ed.), *Simulation in Social Science*, Englewood Cliffs, N. J., Prentice-Hall, 1962, p. 49.

[18] A. Paul Hare, "Computer Simulation of Interaction in Small Groups," *Behavioral Science*, Vol. VI, No. 3, July 1961, p. 265.

[19] John T. Gullahorn and Jeanne E. Gullahorn, "Computers in Behavioral Science," *Behavioral Science*, Vol. VIII, No. 4, October 1963, pp. 354-362.

[20] Russell L. Ackoff, *Scientific Method*, New York, John Wiley and Sons, 1962, p. 108.

[21] Ralph Thomlinson, "A Model for Migration Analysis," *Journal of the American Statistical Association*, Vol. LVI, No. 295, September 1961, pp. 675-686.

[22] Herbert A. Simon, "Some Strategic Considerations in the Construction of Social Science Models," in Paul F. Lazarsfeld (ed.), *Mathematical Thinking in the Social Sciences*, Glencoe, Ill., Free Press, 1954, p. 414.

[23] Nicholas Rashevsky, *Mathematical Theory of Human Relations*, Principia Press, Bloomington, 1947; and *Mathematical Biology of Social Behavior*, Chicago, University of Chicago Press, 1951.

[24] Stuart Carter Dodd, *Dimensions of Society*, New York, The Macmillan Co., 1942.

25 John von Neumann and Oskar Morgenstern, *Theory of Games and Economic Behavior*, Princeton, Princeton University Press, 1947.

26 Irwin D. J. Bross, *Design for Decision*, New York, The Macmillan Co., 1953, pp. 2-4.

27 C. West Churchman, Russell L. Ackoff, and E. Leonard Arnoff, *Introduction to Operations Research*, New York, John Wiley and Sons, 1957, pp. 13-15.

Chapter VII.

1 Samuel A. Stouffer, *Communism, Conformity, and Civil Liberties*, New York, Doubleday & Co., 1955.

2 Gordon W. Allport, *The Nature of Prejudice*, Boston, Beacon Press, 1954.

3 T. W. Adorno, E. Frenkel-Brunswick, D. J. Levinson, and R. N. Sanford, *The Authoritarian Personality*, New York, Harper & Brothers, 1950.

4 Stouffer, *Communism, Conformity and Civil Liberties*, p. 14.

5 *Ibid.*, pp. 250-261.

6 *Ibid.*, pp. 237-238.

7 *Ibid.*, p. 241.

8 *Ibid.*, pp. 247-248.

9 *Ibid.*, pp. 54-55.

10 *Ibid.*, pp. 52-53.

11 *Ibid.*, pp. 110-113.

12 *Ibid.*, pp. 57, 87, 107, 155, 186, 202, and 217.

13 *Ibid.*, p. 220.

Chapter VIII.

1 Henry Pratt Fairchild (ed.), *Dictionary of Sociology*, Ames, Iowa, Littlefield Adams and Co., 1944, p. 302.

2 Morris R. Cohen, *Law and the Social Order*, New York, Harcourt, Brace and Co., 1933, p. 242.

3 Robert K. Merton, *Social Theory and Social Structure*, Glencoe, Ill., Free Press, 1949, pp. 98-101.

4 Elbridge Sibley, *The Education of Sociologists in the United States*, New York, Russell Sage Foundation, 1963, p. 84.

5 Janice Harris Hopper, "To Be a Sociologist," in H. Laurence Ross (ed.), *Perspectives on the Social Order*, New York, McGraw-Hill Book Co., 1963, pp. 452-465.

6 Sibley, *Education of Sociologists*, p. 88.

7 Matilda White Riley, "Membership in the American Sociological Association: 1950-1959," *American Sociological Review*, Vol. XXV, No. 6, December 1960, pp. 916-917.

8 Abbott L. Ferriss, "Sociological Manpower," *American Sociological Review*, Vol. XXIX, No. 1, February 1964, pp. 104-111.

9 *Ibid.*, p. 114.

10 Riley, "Membership in the American Sociological Association," pp. 920-921.

11 *Ibid.*, pp. 923-926.

12 Hornell Hart, "Comparative Coverage of Agreed-on Sociological Topics," Project for Comparative Analysis of Introductory Sociology Textbooks, Third Report, 1959, mimeographed.

13 Raymond Kennedy and Ruby Jo Kennedy, "Sociology in American Colleges," *American Sociological Review*, Vol. VII, No. 5, October 1942, p. 661.

14 Lawrence Podell, Martin Vogelfanger, and Roberta Rogers, "Sociology in American Colleges: Fifteen Years Later," *American Sociological Review*, Vol. XXIV, No. 1, February 1959, p. 89.

15 Robert K. Merton, "The Mosaic of the Behavioral Sciences," in Bernard Berelson (ed.), *The Behavioral Sciences Today*, New York, Harper Torchbooks, 1963, p. 249.

Suggested Reading

*

Anthropology

For a view of how people of other cultures act and think, anthropologists are the best authorities. Brown writes fluently and briefly of many cultures for a general audience, Herskovits and Kroeber are authoritative and encyclopedic, and Murdock presents social practices in statistical tables.

Ina Corinne Brown, *Understanding Other Cultures*, Englewood Cliffs, N. J., Prentice-Hall, 1963 (paperbound).

Melville J. Herskovits, *Man and His Works*, New York, Knopf, 1948.

Alfred Louis Kroeber, *Anthropology*, New York, Harcourt Brace, 1948.

George P. Murdock, *Social Structure*, New York, Macmillan, 1949.

Sociology

Focusing primarily but not exclusively on contemporary European-American society, the following books analyze our own behavior. Berger entertains while informing, Chinoy identifies basic concepts, Davis exemplifies the functional approach, Lundberg and associates offer a widely used introductory textbook, Merton analyzes the interplay between theory and research, and Page discusses the changing role and image of sociology.

Peter L. Berger, *Invitation to Sociology*, New York, Doubleday, 1963 (paperbound).

Ely Chinoy, *Sociological Perspective*, New York, Random House, 1954 (paperbound).

Kingsley Davis, *Human Society*, New York, Macmillan, 1949.

George A. Lundberg, Clarence C. Schrag, and Otto N. Larsen, *Sociology*, New York, Harper and Row, 1963.

Robert K. Merton, *Social Theory and Social Structure*, Glencoe, Ill., Free Press, 1957.

Charles H. Page (ed.), *Sociology and Contemporary Education*, New York, Random House, 1964 (paperbound).

Methodology

Dealing with various aspects of field and other social research, these books require no mathematical knowledge. Hyman discusses interviewing and related techniques, Lundberg explores the positivist underpinning of sociology, and Riley and Selltiz supply reliable examples of textbooks describing formal and informal sociological research.

Herbert H. Hyman, *Survey Design and Analysis*, Glencoe, Ill., Free Press, 1955.

George A. Lundberg, *Foundations of Sociology*, New York, McKay, 1964 (paperbound).

Matilda White Riley, *Sociological Research*, New York, Harcourt Brace and World, 1963.

Claire Selltiz, Marie Jahoda, Morton Deutsch, and Stuart W. Cook, *Research Methods in Social Relations*, New York, Hold-Dryden, 1959.

Statistics

Quantitative work in sociology sometimes requires only simple arithmetic and at other times advanced mathematics; the last two of this set of books are easy, the first two are moderately difficult, and none demands calculus. Dixon and Massey contribute a very competent general textbook, Hansen and associates supply an excellent treatment of sampling principles and procedures, Huff engagingly exposes faulty uses of statistics, and Wallis and Roberts introduce general statistics.

Wilfrid J. Dixon and Frank J. Massey Jr., *Introduction to Statistical Analysis*, New York, McGraw-Hill, 1957.

Morris H. Hansen, William N. Hurwitz, and William G. Madow, *Sample Survey Methods and Theory*, New York, Wiley, 1953.

Darrell Huff, *How to Lie with Statistics*, New York, Norton, 1954.

W. Allen Wallis and Harry V. Roberts, *The Nature of Statistics*, New York, Collier, 1962 (paperbound).

Computers

Large quantities of data call for machine processing, and the following books are among the as yet relatively few describing computer uses pertinent to social science. Bernstein relates the historical development of computers, Flores explains their internal workings, Green addresses himself particularly to behavioral scientists, and Halacy provides a popular treatment of the current scene regarding electronic data processors.

Jeremy Bernstein, *The Analytical Engine*, New York, Random House, 1964.

Ivan Flores, *Computer Logic*, Englewood Cliffs, N. J., Prentice-Hall, 1960.

Bert F. Green Jr., *Digital Computers in Research*, New York, McGraw-Hill, 1963.

Daniel S. Halacy Jr., *Computers: The Machines We Think With*, New York, Dell, 1962 (paperbound).

Applications

The samples below help to show how scientific research can contribute to man's knowledge about himself and the groups to which he belongs. Kemeny and Snell summarize several instances of model-building, Lundberg reflects upon the role that social science may play in shaping the society of the future, Stouffer collects instances of his lifetime of social research, and the final book reports on a case of large-scale field work.

John G. Kemeny and J. Laurie Snell, *Mathematical Models in the Social Sciences*, Boston, Ginn, 1962.

George A. Lundberg, *Can Science Save Us?*, New York, Longmans Green, 1961 (paperbound).

Samuel A. Stouffer, *Social Research to Test Ideas*, Glencoe, Ill., Free Press, 1962.

Samuel A. Stouffer *et al.*, *The American Soldier: Studies in Social Psychology in World War II*, Princeton, Princeton University Press, 4 vols., 1949-1950.

Periodicals

Numerous professional journals publish sociological articles, of which the following are among the best. A.J.S. (to use the customary abbreviation) commands considerable respect, A.S.R. is the official organ of the American Sociological Association, J.A.S.A. is the foremost statistics journal publishing sociological articles, and S.A. systematically digests articles and books related to sociology in all languages (abstracts grouped into 22 areas of specialization are available as "Information Files").

American Journal of Sociology, Chicago, 6 issues a year, since 1895.

American Sociological Review, Washington, 6 issues a year, since 1936.

Journal of the American Statistical Association, Washington, 4 issues a year, since 1906.

Sociological Abstracts, New York, 8 issues a year, since 1953.

Index

*